WHEN THE
NEXT BIG WAR
BLOWS DOWN
THE VALLEY

WHEN THE NEXT BIG WAR BLOWS DOWN THE VALLEY

Selected and New Poems

Terese Svoboda

Tallahassee, Florida • 2015

Cover art and design: Jay Snodgrass
Author Photo: Claire Holt
Text design and production: Carol Lynne Knight
Type Styles: text set in ITC Veljovic and titles set in Trajan Pro

Library of Congress Cataloging-in-Publication Data
When the Next Big War Blows Down the Valley: Selected and New Poems by Terese Svoboda, First Edition
ISBN – 978-1-934695-45-6
Library of Congress Cataloging Card Number – 2015941657

Anhinga Press Inc. is dedicated wholly to the publication and appreciation of fine poetry and other literary genres.

For personal orders, catalogs and information write to:
Anhinga Press
P.O. Box 3665
Tallahassee, Florida 32315
Website: www.anhingapress.org
Email: info@anhinga.org

Published in the United States
by Anhinga Press
Tallahassee, Florida
First Edition, 2015

To Stephen Medaris Bull, muse and ironist

CONTENTS

NEW: ALL THE LIVELONG DAY

Acknowledgments

My most heartfelt gratitude to those presses that originally published the selected poems: University of Arkansas Press, University of Iowa Press, University of Georgia Press, and Zoo Press.

My thanks to the journals where these poems first appeared, sometimes in a different version.

Agni: "Sister Love"

Altered Scale Gallery: "Apassionata"

American Poetry Review: "For They Know Not What They Do," "Fitting In," "Marriage Boat"

Atlantic: "Aubade"

Boston Review: "Harp and the Machine," "The Convoy Never Moves," "Fuel Adieu"

Boulevard: "The Ranchhand's Daughter"

Cabin Fever: Poets at Joaquin Miller's Cabin: 1984-2001 (Word Works): "How to Simplify Fractions"

Columbia: "At the Castle"

Cortland Review: "Cycles"

Degrees of Freedom: "Jean/Jeanne Baret"

Devouring the Green: The Cyborg Lyric Anthology (Jaded Ibis Productions): "Devouring the Green," "Please Please Me," "The Wait," "Flavor"

Diagram: "Rock 'n Roll," "So Not Dead"

Field: "Bridge, Mother," "Rule of K"

Georgia Review: "A Moo from a Can with a Cow on It"

Hotel Amerika: "Picnic Portents," "Code Name: 731" as "731"

IOU: New Writing on Money (Concord Free Press): "Money Standing Around"

Kenyon Review: "Septic Conversation"

Little Star: "Seasoned"

Massachusetts Review: "Crucifixion" and "All Aberration"

Narrative: "Odysseus's Mother-in-Law"

The Nation: "Picnic," "Crash-and-a-Half"

New Letters: "Sonnet"

New Republic: "Karon" as "Sharon" and "Bird Boy"

New World Writing: "Toodles"

New Yorker: "Pink," "The Root of Father is Fat"

Open City: "Dove-Whirr"

Paris Review: "High School Report," "Rock Polisher," "Eurydice Abandoned in the Caves of Hades," "Sex and Class and Race," "Inventor," "Aphra Plays," "The Root of Mother is Moth"

Pequod: "I Kissed Thee Ere I Killed Thee," "No Historical Marker"

Ploughshares: "Dog in the Wall," "Money Can't Fix It," "Obscenity," "Philomel," "Laughing Africa," "Secret Executions of GIs/Black by GIs/White in Occupied Japan" as "Secret Executions of Black GIs in Occupied Japan," "Public Works"

Plume: "Riviera Terrors" and "Antigone Wins"

Plume Anthology: "The Terraces Against the Hillside Say Immortal, the Trees —"

Poetry: "Hairy Streams"

Poetry Daily: "Susurrus of Sheets, Goodbye"

Poetry International: "Common Good"

Prairie Schooner: "Driving L.A.," "Root Canal as a Venetian Idyll," "When the Next Big War Blows Down the Valley," "Skinny Dip"

Salamagundi: "Unicorn"

Significant Objects: "Heart-Shaped Candle Romance"

The Southampton Review: "There's a Closet for That"

Times Literary Supplement: "My Mature Style"

Valparaiso Poetry Review: "Octopus"

Virginia Quarterly Review: "Barking Dogs"

Verse: "Statues of Women That are Neither Angels Nor Allegory"

Yale Review: "Orpheus," "Death Stayed," and "Slave Children"

"As the Birds," reprinted from *Laughing Africa* in *Drive, They Said* (Milkweed Editions)

"Bridge, Mother" reprinted in *Poetry Daily*

"Bridge, Mother," "Pink" and "Secret Executions of GIs/Black by GIs/White in Occupied Japan" as "Secret Executions of Black GIs in Occupied Japan" reprinted in *Witness* (Jackleg Press)

"Cowboy" reprinted in *Logan House Anthology of 21st Century American Poetry* (Logan House Press)

"Report from High School," reprinted in *Red, White & Blue Vistas on the Promise of America* (University of Iowa Press)

"When the Next Big War Blows Down the Valley" reprinted in *Poem of the Day*

Very big thanks to Stephanie Strickland, Felix Bull, Frank Bull, Kalin Mitchev, Maureen Seaton, Mary Sherman Willis, Eleanor Wilner, the late Nell Altizer, Enid Shomer, Robert Levy, Neil de la Flor, Nancy Schoenberger, Mary Stewart Hammond, the Corporation of Yaddo, the MacDowell Colony, the Rockefeller Foundation Bellagio Center, the Liguria Study Center, Ossabaw, and the Writers Room. Lynne Knight, Kristine Snodgrass and Jay Snodgrass, yes!

WHEN THE NEXT BIG WAR BLOWS DOWN THE VALLEY

We play until Death calls us in.

— KURT SCHWITTERS

SELECTED

I. THE CONVOY NEVER MOVES

BAIYER RIVER, PAPUA NEW GUINEA

The road stops, not in a suburban cul-de-sac
but where the bulldozer's sunk.
Thirty or so men mill at the wreck

in shorts and Coke or Sony T-shirts.
They all have shoes and guns. Dirt
from the *plantesin* seams their skin. The Hertz

rent-a-jeep is theirs, as far as we're concerned.
Last year a missionary, in terror-turned-
bravado, ran a roadblock and disappeared,

and he brought immortality
to the valley — penicillin — which is why
the road got this far, the only

reason. Soon-to-be-extinct butterflies
flutter in pools of urine by
the roadside where they strategize —

for us, for anyone. The road must pay.
Two men wear grass skirts, try to say
our names, as the rest do not. Are they

less hostile because we're their dinner?
To eat means *to exploit* to all consumers.
Beyond the misty range before us, copper

and gold-capped mountains alchemize
men wearing neckties and Levi's
into Cortez, astride big machines.

Meanwhile,
because it is always meanwhile
back at the pass for someone, all

these night-of-the-living-dead men strip
the jeep, even take the contract and rip
it up for rolling paper, which is when *If*

this, then — hits home. Why us?
Our T-shirts spell out outrageousness
in their blankness.

We take off the shirts, our shoes.
If it's not their road, whose
is it? And why so dangerous?

THE ANSWERS

The President nauseates.

The cell gets banned, *gets*
verbs its way into the body,
begets.
                    Bush-amped, the President
cuts his tongue.

                    Propagation.
But phony, that tongue,
21 million of them, wireless
unless the President throws up

his hands at blood.

What an explosion!
Each cell has its say:
each to his own, each,
then, disposes.

                    The President
makes us sick. See cells
by the seaside? You
call in the answers.

SLAUGHTER OF THE CENTAURS

Woods, glades, copses, massed oak,
the vines of Atreus, trillium,
dogbane, an excess of green,
the insects cryptic with cold,
green with a fine English

mist that softens the streaks
of blood glistening on the flanks
of the coarsely forelocked boys,
none more than fifteen,
beardless, death

catching them cantering,
berets cocked, weapons not.
See the tattoos on their chests,
the mermaid's swinging hair,
the laughing snake? They went

as we will. See the strong hooves
still twitching? The warm earth,
ravaged in reflex? But they were
warriors, planted in their mothers'
wombs for nothing else,

their beautiful tails curled
around their wet bellies,
lifted, so delicately, to fan
the light. Brighter now, you can see
boys in wrecked jeeps in camouflage.

UNIT 731

a/k/a Epidemic Prevention and Water Purification Department
with special code Maruta *for humans.*

A lumber mill is what they said it was
where the logs — live GIs —
lost their lungs without going under
      to the Japanese whitecoats they thought
      would treat them.
                    Or were amputated to observe
blood loss.
Or limbs attached to the other side. Or intact limbs frozen
and used
to study rotting.

Raped for syphilis studies.

      And for the Chinese: cholera, plague, anthrax
dropped as bombs.
          Half million dead.

Poisoned food and candies for the children.
Grenades tested, flame throwers, germ-releasing bombs.
People centrifuged, buried alive.

Studied.

     I was afraid during my first vivisection, but the second time
around, it was much easier. — Ken Yuasa, 2007.

A dragon steps forward in big flame, mushroom smoke and
      add to this, fawning. Stomach talk: US and Tokyo.
Weeds
                  occupy
the world. Is there sense to that?

We bought the files:
infants, elderly, pregnant women, us.

To yet slay the field's dragons — so many —
          grief airs itself as joke.
                        The geisha,
with only four toes on each foot, circled
     a *wee wee wee* all the way home.

          Or else planted the GIs bone and vial,
          dug in
     quick before the Occupation,
          wild mustard in a crack.

Only the shoes left,
I am happy to say, just the horror. Blood on the shoes.
But the buildings were too good,
     and stood.

     The geisha's toes go just over the bones,
the dragons' teeth all maimed warriors,
               the field's so green beyond and besides —
               B-sides of that tune —
monster Mothra's egg hatches
in the dirt,
the mother pooping them then
             webbing away into the sunrise/set,
leaving them living.

Cyanide capsules post-war, for all medical personnel.

          Yet nothing stays buried —
surely hyperbole — where doubt digs. Sidereal time slips,

stomachs talk and now we feel all those dendrons,
boneless nerve sites, sighting old dragons,

                                        citing lot
                    and footnote of where
                            the Japanese nurse worked
who helped bury the bodies
                            and their pieces,
on the grounds,
no geisha an octogenarian who tells you
            your toes, your little held back giggle ready-to-launch

pigs big and little, none alien, all-American,
arrested no one, and bought the files.
                    So what if the Russians objected —
that was communist propaganda.

            We bought the files. How much cold can a body take?
How little liver?
                    Where to stand for the flame's throw?
                            Mental patients given trials of poison,
no trial.
In the 90's

731's Dr. Ryoichi Naito, who handed over such secrets,
            founded Green Cross
                            that distributed AIDS-laden blood
for transfusions.

            Boys' sawn bones turn up in the Tokyo lot.

No Historical Marker

An anthropologist takes us
to the highest point of
Waiheke Island, New Zealand.

Anything high, to quote Eliade, hooks up
to God. *But,* she says, *there's also
the intoxication of subjugation,*

if only the meadow to the mountain.
This gigantic midden of oyster shell, fishbone,
and ash — trash, really — islanders call *pa.*

We climb it. Surely some jadeslung Maori,
nobly romantic or at least strong
from heaving boulders over the edge,

lifts us to his feathered shoulders:
it's exactly that high. The vista's
two more islands, the serifs

of twenty flagged sailboats,
the ripples of whales, a rosary of sheep.
We whoop: *This is paradise.*

To that, birds crash through the low ferns
ingloriously, scandalizing their species
but trilling an apology so musical

it's obvious why they're spared extinction.
Then one fern goes on fluttering.
It's the little people — a race

felled (like Ireland's) by clubs,
a harvest maybe a jot more humane
than that of jeans and beer.

The fright pulls us down the side,
flapping like the birds weighting
the trees, already aroost in the dusk.

Christ, she says, pouring tea,
why should it be the moa that
haunts visitors the most?

A Moo from a Can with a Cow on It

The last dolphin won't save us.
The bombs strapped to his back
must sink him. The turtles
never return once they reach

the pavement. Some musk (creosote?)
drives them — like us
in the Toyota, our limbs withdrawn,
in line for the on-ramp.

You can get all the endangered
stuffed, in bright colors,
but the baby turns towards
the birds every time, rapt.

What will he turn to later?
Peck, peck, peck — a toy
that dips forever? A moo
from a can with a cow on it?

In Kansas the last moose
kneels to the hunter. There is
a sound when you twist the trophy
from the body. They think

it's not speech that separates us,
but foresight. Listen
as the kittens are pulled
from the teat to the toilet.

Obscenity

Obscenity is often not an expression uttered by an individual under great stress and condemned as bad taste, but one permitted and even prescribed by society.
— E. Evans-Pritchard,
British social anthropologist, 1925

Among the Ba-Ila,
among as if swarming
the petri dish of the British
Imperialist,

there exist expressions used collectively,
that is, in the presence
of women and children,
in fact, in chorus

since these obscenities
are sung, not scrawled
across a riverbank
where innocent boaters

of Victorian persuasion
might encounter them.
His great penis is a size!
A thing without end!

It must have a long unwinding!
The female mourner's song,
the trot arch as if the words
themselves might make

the gored warrior rise in tumescence.
Sometimes it's just what they do
with their hands, singing,
writes the patrician scientist

who considered obscenity
a privilege, a way to spur
routine labor with ardor,
or to invoke life

at the moment of death. I drag in
the anthropological so one can reject
the paradigm of the primitive,
we who have no physical labor

which requires our neighbor,
nor sustained interest in creation —
except in art, that work
to ward off death.

There will always be those
in the boat who slow down,
who listen and transcribe
in their tiny script.

THE DEAD DANCE

The winds were headed straight at us for days before and during the test.
— GLEN CURBOW, FORMER RONGERIK WEATHER UNIT COMMANDER
FOR BRAVO, THE LARGEST OF THE 300 H-BOMBS EXPLODED
OVER THE PACIFIC

I

Polynesia seemed just a fifth-grade
dalliance in sticky crepe paper or,
at most, the prom's promise, an upright fan
blowing against a cardboard palm

when I flew there, so hip to the sixties'
four-letter love that the two men
caught coupling in the plane's john
were, at most, amusing. But that first morning,

waking not only to the ardent rooster
but to two goats soldered
to each other, then changing
money, the prim Queen on one side,

Tangaroa on the other, all member,
then blocked from breakfast
by a parade where the figure
on the float pumped watery milk

all over the cheering crowd,
I clutched at my pills.
Too dazzled by sex for promiscuity,
still learning *a* to *b*

memorizing the Kama Sutra,
my education wasn't that catholic.
You stinky vagina! one kid shouted
to another. *You bent penis!*

While one's first translations
aren't always the most profound,
preoccupations tell: Eskimos, snow,
Africans, cows; Americans, cars.

The back of the rat goes up and down.
The P.M.'s son, a darker Charles Laughton,
is his brother's father. This,
what we call the last husk, shucked.

II

Ah, the noble savage who is
neither. I go dancing that night.
Rather, I buy a drink and the women's
swaying raffia advances on me,

the drumming men turn all insistence,
daring me to do what all my adolescent
jerks, dirty dogs, limbos
had not prepared me for.

Circle by circle, my crude motions
lose all innocence, and they
laugh, mimic me, laugh again.
It's the song that suggests

more depth: *Pan America*,
named after the plane
that burned over Tahiti,
dancer-full. A twitching

sadness it is, in a slightly minor
key, a tragedy to dance to.
We yell at the end, touched,
erotic, thankful.

III

Palms broom the yard, flailing
with spray that's more than rain,
a typhoon's air-and-ocean.

Two chickens fight for shelter
under a pawpaw. Whichever loses is dinner.
Ngarima twirls her machete until the storm's

all fluff, and out of this haze zigzags
Preacher Vatu in a football helmet.
He raps his knuckle against its vinyl:

Coconuts in this wind can kill you.
We sip hot tea on our haunches
as the chicken grills, but he won't wait

to eat. *A miscarriage to attend.*
He tips his head toward the mountain.
Before, I didn't bother.

Out beyond the pawpaw stands the fence,
every inch flowers. Here, where a twig drops,
there's a tree tomorrow.

IV

Polynesia's ghosts are not forgotten.
At night the dogs howl for their kind,

roasting in the *umu*, cut down in packs
by cars, the island's thinnings.

I almost miss their smokeless oven,
walk over one and think it's only clots

of pulsing lava. The ghosts of humans seep
from the broken crypts, the limestone

paper-flimsy against hibiscus or the thick
poison roots of manioc. *The dead*

must dance, one moon-gold boy
insists. I witness a funeral:

begun in propriety, matching dresses,
dark slacks, white shirts, straw hats,

then someone sings, and by the chorus
two women are doing pew-side what to them

is pure offering, to us, lust. The spiritual
can never equal the scent of *tipani,*

a blood-heat climate, the body's pleasure,
a glide across a plate-flat lagoon.

Once you die, you're as good as a radio
left out in the rain or a cassette unstrung —

hardly rewarded. No, the dead want back
and those athwart the graves, coupling

under canopies of mats, try to persuade them
otherwise, crying out over love-thrusts.

V

But a miscarriage mourned?
Here everyone gets a baby, even
single young men, largesse from women

with over ten, *succes d'estime.*
It is amusing, that primitive measure.
More than amusing. Vili twists

a teenager's arm so I can see the marks.
I make some tests to stop the babies.
I tell them be modern, it's like Coke,

this vaccination. When I finish
I get a ticket to Switzerland, land
of leather shorts. Can you believe it?

All for me, some new packet of birth control,
a month's barrenness. For that each woman's
promised an equivalent mirror or matches,

TV or stove. Or less.
They don't know. I leave after six months
with reasons not as recondite

as Bligh's. *Paradise?*
That went out with colonial
appellation, New this, New that,

says some soured missionary
in the museum. In front of me,
every Tangaroa's penis-less.

VI

Ten years after the airport
farewell, the sports team singing
as their ladies shushushed
their skirts to *Pan America*,

I'm so much smarter.
I know the miscarriage was a jelly baby,
one of many born in secret,
with transparent twitching organs only,

or worse, a live monster with rolling
eyes, few limbs, half-human cries,
some women now with seven tries.
Think Krakatoa,

that Polynesian Apocalypse, that atoll
explosion that gave Europe
its first sunset beauty, the decor
for Mann's beaches, a *fin de siécle*

ornament, then think bigger, think
BRAVO, American self-congratulation
twenty-five-miles-high planned
to test the people of Paradise,

then three hundred more mushrooms
cracking the atolls, dusting
the children in yellow, burning spore.
Instead of milkspray from a homemade god,

the half-life of a juggernaut, ON
THE BEACH on the beach. Sold
to protect hot showers, Mercedes,
above-ground swimming pools,

and our new babies.
Yes, ours have finally arrived,
the boom of this generation
of equal size, our dalliance with sex

only a decade's fad. I know
so much more now. Such as:
how the sunset bleeds the world over,
how the palms bend at that hackneyed angle

with the same breeze that sways
the willows over Hackensack,
how the waves carry the wastes to me,
how they're all our babies.

CRUCIFIXION

Eighty-eight people, including two children ... sentenced to death
by hanging or crucifixion in Sudan.
— ALLAFRICA.COM, AUGUST 27, 2002

It's nonfiction,
a newspaper's open and shut.
But make that *suffocation*,
it's more genteel, the way

the limbs fail the lungs.
You want to read *a hill*
full of crosses but
Khartoum has no hills,

it's flat desert.
And it's not nails for the hands
and feet — it's staples.
Big staples. People prefer

the touch of technology.
Besides, you have to be angry
to pound, or have a lot of energy.
Who, in this heat? They're

all just criminals anyway,
or political prisoners,
Shell employees. There's
something about a post hole digger

working a cross into place
and the cross recycled,
the wood old — blood-sticky,
sandy, the flies.

Only occasionally do they
attach a footrest
to make it last longer.
Only occasionally

do they cut them down
and put them up the next day.
Only occasionally
are there no birds.

Pollution is catching up though.
Soon no scarlet-tailed hawks
or owls with tinfoil claws.
But who believes this?

UNICORN

As men, to try the precious unicorn's horn,
Make of the powder a preservative circle,
And in it put a scorpion.
— JOHN WEBSTER, *THE WHITE DEVIL*

A scorpion struts through the ring of powder,
then dies.

In Britain, 300 years ago, the scorpion
        was certainly as rare
as the unicorn but its death
        proved the unicorn lived.
                But had died, of course,

its horn being ground to powder
                which is white like
        the white rhino's,

white like what the girl from Amsterdam's
                licking off her mirror,

and now the rhino's rare. We think the girl's alive.

Then too, men pondered over
                the bones of the triceratops,
                        labeling them
        the blasted dragon's
ears. And ground them for sex.

                        It's no wonder Mattel
turns out a pink synthetic-maned unicorn
to fetch the eight-year-old virgins,
                our best specimens.

Or that it took Lincoln seven hours to die.
That is, the twenty surgeons
packed into the small dressing room could cut
as well as ours but had no drugs.

He was a rare man
to proclaim emancipation, even under pressure,
to free black from white
even if that's still a matter of myth.

Such is progress:
the scorpion rising on its many legs, coming to,

and the unicorn
spread before the roaring fire

where the Dutch girl lolls, empowdered.

FOR THEY KNOW NOT WHAT THEY DO

There are soldiers in Mother's hair
and soldiers peeling the screen.
Distracted? I am driven.
I can't stop this chattering
with history hissing its heat.

Grave raincoat-shouldered people
with their own histories, bad
histories, drink to their bitterness
and chide us for our efforts.
What is there other than *I forget?*

I can't read the papers, or your face
on the phone. *Give it up* is the answer, *is*
is the answer, *aghast* is the hair.
The rain's washed off most of our skin.
How does it feel during a war?

A silence stirs.

TRAINS IN THE DARK

Split from space, time-launched but time-less,
our car carries night itself. There's a through line

between apocalypse and shock, that word
coined when trains first carried man past beast.

We're post, the bomb's gone off a hundred times
a hundred, the soup of it invisible in our breath,

not even fog against the pane, this soup the train
drives into, end game. The post modern,

post feminist, post digital, post/pillar/post — the whistle's
already blown, we're shocked, sliding mercury-like

between rails in a soup of space uniting time and trouble:
Middle East, North Korea, Sudan ready in the tender —

the posts we pass hold upturned boots,
the posts — those blurred flashes — all khaki.

COWBOY

The rez was a strip of light
I'd hitchhiked not far enough into.
Already the stubble held the down
of the next snowfall and the moon's

albumen, and no one drove by.
Until, like the opening shot where a car
seems to float in one place, it came,
unspooling in size, not one rise

between us, just sky. I jumped up
and down on the middle line to stop
those fifteen Sioux in a coupe,
a carnival ride. They had room.

But what they had left of their names
was not Sioux: John Steele,
Henrietta Sells, and Sean, the baby,
whose mouth kept kissing the air.

Was Moon-in-the-Hair better?
Or Yellow Snake? Oliver, the squinter,
a speeder, our driver, took up talking:
I was ten, old enough to be done

playing Indian. Whoever done?
sang someone in reprise from the backseat.
We all laughed. Oliver knocked
the wipers on. *My brother Albert —*

the name shushed them all — *showed me*
how to tie the knot, the knot
for the lynching part. I was the one
who hauled up the rope, the only one

big enough. A handful of snow blew
up from the vent. *Well, somebody*
had to be cowboy. We slid off
the road a ways, hitting ice,

then slid back. *Some say Indians*
got nothing. I say we got a load.
To die a white man's death.
He shook his head. *In Nam,*

I shot a kid in the face
who had a grenade tied to his waist
and his face was Albert's.
That time I knew

what I did, or thought so.
But I waited too long. He popped out
one fake blue eyeball and handed it,
woman by woman, to me. *Next time*

l kill for whitey, it had better be
suicide. He giggled away, steering
with his chest, opening the sixth
of a six-pack. I couldn't complain.

He took me clear into dawn,
to a truck stop where I could see,
over coffee, halfway across the state,
how snow lay over most of it.

VERY FORGETFUL

Lincoln lounges in Obama's chair.
The clang and whoop of party din —

of actual people, not plastic politicians —
is braced for by a guard

with a flashlight, lantern-type: *Hope*.
Obama and his girls stand in the dark,

Booth in the shadows. *Carpe diem?*
The sun does rise again.

Washington's obelisk rises too,
billowing burnt fuel, virtually

starbound, the only firework.
We forget how the rational ennobles.

MONEY CAN'T FIX IT

My eyes must be open because light
through the woof of the hut's weave
shows my arm in pin shivers. What
wakes me?

      A howl unfolds outside,
Fear-in-the-mouth, a breathing trill
certifying the silence after. Sheep
in a barn as flimsy as mine

drum panic that my bones pick up,
an arthritis of fear. I stand, or at least
the dark and sleep leave on another level,
      that kind of attention.

      My story is half-heard and resented
in a bar where A-7 has played fierce
as a drill since midnight, where now
someone breaks something

      and even the guy on my left
stops with his hands. When the cry comes,
there's this blip in the neon
            we all watch.

          Money can't fix it
says the jukebox, going on
while the glass gets swept.

I Kissed Thee Ere I Killed Thee

— Othello

The moon drops. The sirens clutch their one note.
Night is a lidded pit where our arms
brush neither stars nor soot.
We feel our breasts, the tips rise, alarmed,
as out there some pitched god swaggers, unsheathed
and mewing, the tenor of which turns and stops
her whom our embarrassed coughs only strop
her fascination. She wants to take the napped head
and rub. He unfolds, the skin the sheen of lead

and dismisses her, considering little
the enormity of her ardor, pulps
the fruit with his one godlike stance, the sibyl's
untoward grimace his. Night riddles
her as she climbs his dark limbs
with sex, all its riptide rhythms
shutting off night and day, the usual order
but here night is bigger, the moon's a supernova.

Here a millennia of famine turns to
conflagration until the hoary lean-to
on an African island comes to stand for
all pleasure. A hunger for mirrors
blackens the backs of stars.
She wriggles free, unharmed, a pregnancy
surely. We croon behind her,
a chorusing Pleiades.

What subsumes this? Nothing's
ignored in that vast flat place, the world,
each ridge marks a falling, each sidling
scrabble a break in lovemaking.
Better, who asks this to be? The quiet woman,
the priapic salesman of color? No one
denies the grip of the generative,
the live
jet emptying. The wheat comes up
and it's morning, the sex stopped.

WHEN THE NEXT BIG WAR
BLOWS DOWN THE VALLEY

Flame casts the overhang in shadow
so no one can see anyone behind the clubs
or sharpened sticks each has made for himself
in the boredom of the many dusks when
the spilt blood has dried or sunk into
the red dirt at the bottom where food
grows and women dance and trees promise
drums and from where no one

ever escapes but takes up
the broken sharpened sticks and cuts
rows into the freshened earth until all they remember
of those from before is their small size,
and not their own good luck.

SECRET EXECUTIONS OF GIS/BLACK BY GIS/WHITE IN OCCUPIED JAPAN

The world yesterday,
its white shoes at the paper door
        — I mean the MP's white gloves of innocence —
no mud in and no one steals
a giant MP's shoes
just the geisha drugs herself into another tenderness
where, a half century on,
        Mr. Rushmore
will rise in one-third size,
in concrete.

        The MPs arrest (memory)
a whole country
when few knew
mushroom bloom
to outstrip the lilac.
        Our soldiers sat in
their Zeroes after,
        wings and fuselage kamikaze-silent
in long rows
under
cherry trees.

        I don't remember that, my uncle says.
All those months move together so many years
        gone:
        the red-furred dog he tamed,
his left-behind baby, the words —

Why did he do it?

O Kyochan, your long silk sleeve
brushing his brow
and strange speech covering the synapse

with idiot noise
          which masks —

O Mothra, so Mother, so monster,
your wings over the egg,
save us too.

      My uncle guarded the postwar's worst,
                        worse after
        the military's who-do-you-think-you-are
                                  here
after the war is over — black?

           kept GIs
in twenty-foot holes dug
      into the frozen ground,
covered with sewer lids,
          or in sit-down cages, i.e.,
you can't stand up and you can't
sit down
              for hours,
in a prison where GI beat GI
(they could, not ought)
      and the winter lasted, nuclear or not,
      a naught no child could grasp,
nor the rah-rah U.S. recruits, their sleeves
            soon thick
       with insignia.

         MacArthur was God and King,
a man all capitals
with a face-mask as heavy
      as a Kwakiutl's,
someone you don't ever know enough about.
Born old in Little Rock,

                    he used bayonets
          on retreating WWI vets
camped beside the Capitol
in 1932.

In 1945
was worshipped,
          but not by Truman.

Black GIs jive marching one-two, one-and-a-two
Black GIs prodded by white MPs to —

Suicide is the option
for the MP too-old-to-remember

                    but first the country plays
its screengame:
                    Weapons Grade,
the blood
                    so frozen, a stick of blood
you have to wedge
in before
time's up,
          where oil spews,
          and palms flare.

                    Will the MPs
who took those pictures, e.g., an iced
                              person of color
          bashed bruised wrapped in plastic,
                              kill themselves?

Good war, bad war, black/white, zero/one war.

Sick of blood, the white gloves,
                              the shoes
tracking it in, the dog tracking
tenderness, the paper door — blackness.
There's a drug.

Mind his car,
its vanishing, a Toyota built
                    out of war,
driven to suicide.
                    Abu Grave?

              In Tokyo his captain had a gallows
        built by Japanese carpenters.
              Even Korean vets spoke of it.
                          No Tyburn Tree
where King Henry's 70,000 hanged but
                              American.

              Fluorescence de jour,
a white lit bulb (not the black to dance to)
on not off on not off

        the rope coiled in an O that says
Say Can You See? what the century
is made of.
                    Just placeholders,
        Suzie Wong's nipples. GIs.

    Arrest those overwrought.
No one else remembers when all the zeroes were
                    nooses, all the ones stepped up.

We wear the mask of the guy who did it —
the present.

LAUGHING AFRICA

Nights in the barn, the clean astringence of urine
steaming into the tendrils of a dungfire, the cattle

sleeping their own way, and me mine, despite the puppies
tied to the housepost, their lean mother snapping, the only window

stuffed with straw. *To keep out snakes?*
No. Reic shifts at watch.

To block the cuckold's spear from the lover's heart.
But once I hear low-flying planes and once a helicopter

comes chop-chopping over this basket of a barn
and Reic lifts his ancient rifle, practically

a blunderbuss, and says, *Of course bullets come right through.*
I imagine seeing his wife's breast bleed as she runs,

the wisps of straw catching fire, the lover, Reic,
his children running slant into the suddenly windy savannah.

There is this laugh that Reic makes, the time he finds
a guerrilla stuffed inside a dead cow. *How could you do this?*

he laughs, *I have so many to feed. Couldn't you hide
behind some bush instead of the stomach of my cow?*

And then he roars, and the strength of it is the measure
of his misfortune. Today Reic and all the people who fed me

are starving, the last Red Cross plane just now downed,
every passenger shot. But what's two million Sudanese?

Nothing to you. To me, it's Reic's clasp multiplied —
not diminished to facelessness, or the archetype of a Grimm tale.

It's Nyapuok rubbing her back with sand, Nyabel grinding grain,
sinuous against rock and water, little Lam checking my breasts

for color, Pel singing to his sister, and that laugh,
that laugh. True, they only fed me once a day,

but it was their only meal. And even if it were the last
fowl beaten from the bush by a string of hungry children,

I ate it, my hunger the first inescapable experience
I'd ever had, mine and no other's. I sucked the stones

of the tamarind and felt lucky, and the touch of malaria
that shook the food on my spoon, and the diarrhea

turned dysentery that drove me away, with excuses, midmeal,
and whatever it was that hurt the gut even when I did eat

(was it worms? the kind you sugar a cut for so they come
crawling out of the wound?) were only the discomforts

of the initiate, the stupid. *What kind of snake was it?*
I point to the black foot of a man already black.

Not poisonous, he says, limping into the sunset,
if I live till morning. And he laughs, walking into

a bloody horizon clean of everything, even the stumps of trees,
and it is not that he dies but that his figure grows smaller.

The Greeks were almost African.

⌒⤴

I hear Africa singing, sable and onyx,
chants in a language more alien to me

than even Homer's, and what I see is Africa
the beautiful, a wilderness that's America's

no longer, its light the one photographers
call blessed, its plains still purple

to the earth's core, its arid canyons split
like skulls for man's first upright grasp.

Atrocities in the Garden of Eden?
As if nudity made people simpler

or children sweetened the limepit.

There is no translation for *machinegun*
and what they use is not pidgin. In the bush

the smallest boys spit on clay replicas,
metal-black and shiny, and then shoot rounds

of wet stinging nettle at each other,
like our children. And in the dusk, one young man asks:

Are you my bride? The CIA promised me a woman.
I don't ask what he did, what betrayal warranted such reward.

What I do know is that there's oil under Wau,
though UPI reports the slaughter's North vs. South, Black/Arab.

Oil instead of slaves, both *ultra vires,*
worth any number of lives. Fifty years ago men met

in a clearing and bashed each other over the head with clubs,
causing no casualties. We sold the guns,

and like the British, whose Sheffield steel
made a fortune selling tomahawks,

we too may reap in coarse design
as in a film from Niger, where Africans disembark

Pan Am in cowboy costume and Marilyn Monroe truck
and re-create the panoply of us and them to ask:

Why do you wear clothes if not to hide your guns?

For them, children are the only immortality.
Mothers walked forty miles thinking me a nurse,

and spit at my trivial interest in their songs.
But we don't believe in children —

they are had like chickenpox, and gotten over.
Nor do we believe in immortality,

a juvenile pre-Freudian fixation,
nor in the pleasure of living every day

for the pleasure of it. We believe work makes us safe,
or love, some four-letter word.

Oh, the women are laughing now, their children
light in their arms. I can imagine

my own little Felix, all his four years
and heavy big-boy boots in my arms, swallowing,

swallowing — but the empathy stinks,
goes coy with metaphor, evades by fingering, by taming the horror

into mere minutes of my time. I know nothing.
Out in their dark, the real dark without a moon

or anything electrical, comes lightning as long as the Nile,
and it silences the milling hungry people,

the way it used to when I bore witness.
The ants of god they call themselves.

What does that make me?

REPORT FROM HIGH SCHOOL

Where they sell greeting cards for jail
and use cops to keep kids in
who've already been *in*, where I write:

Security is terrible and they can only spell
food, where just the super stays
for more than three months —

Why not write about me?
asks the teenager with few teeth
and a smile to prove it.

There's a monster after me.
The bathroom's on fire, the tap's all gas
and rat guts and what I need

is a glass of water.
Yesterday the CIA recruited.
They want us and they'll give us

a roof to watch from.
Suck Sambo. The fire licking the dark
reflects us exactly. Write that.

KOMODO DRAGON

You can get there only from Kuala Lumpur, not Timor.
Few Timorese since we exterminated them
     in '74,
         the masked invasion only a minor inconvenience
     to air travelers to Bali,
one which left no survivors but what they call *pirates*,
         people who once had homes and thieves of
their own.

No survivors. Once on Komodo, you'll see the dragons,
saved from god-knows-what interplanetary winter
     of casual radiation.
         They wallow in hot estuaries
     but do not spew fire.
Man had to invent that, unable to accept how
         the term *cold-blooded* weds us.

I'm thinking now of the Tasmanians, other island-dwellers.
When the English landed, those proto-anthropologists,
     justice lovers,
         and Benthamites, they slaughtered all
     but ten of them. The survivors sat

for a photo wearing borrowed spats and leg o'muttons,
         looking like Cro-Magnon acceding to Homo
         Sapien.

In Komodo, the Japanese men with their long lenses seem
voyeuristic in intent
and the bleak quonset huts with their orange
     and green plastic
         dragons, casts of footprints,
     photos of various half-eaten
carcasses, minus the flies, prepare one
         for similar cheapness.

But at 120 degrees and every inch beyond the blind
teeming with hand-wide spiders, vipers with beige eyes,
          and double-tined
                    nits dragging proboscis elephant-size,
          one demands more than special effects.
And the animal (reptiles are still
                              animals) rewards. Its feeding, that tear

and rip and gulp, is ecstasy — who could forget
the low hiss, the avian skittering,
          the delicate
                    tasting, touching, smelling tongue,
          how it alarmed one, especially this last,
like a nervous predilection, or worse,
                    a licking of the lips.

Yards of innards float forth, almost out of view,
that of a pony, or some surprised sleeping native,
          and cockatoo
                    cruise the offal
          with sea eagles, and friar birds.

Half the dragon's life is a bird's, lounging in the lontar
                    palm until its weight breaks the nearly
hollow tree.
Then it trots back through the bush and digs burrows.
Until 1912 no one knew they existed.
          That is,
                    no one who counted, meaning
                    no colonial. Imagine the dragons swimming up,
the researcher at his washing.
                    And how the reptiles survived when
others died

is all mystery. Most likely they just drifted
along on their crack of land, their persistence
      as undirected
          as ours will be,
     given our propensity to let things slide.
Mutation, that's the ticket.
                    We'll have a dream about Raymond Burr

skeptical of Godzilla's arrival
amid the nuclear rubble and then wake up
      to find
          what we're dying of
     is not the usual cancer, that we're just growing
more arms, all of us well on our way
          to becoming Shiva.

Or Kali. Would bestiality be better?
With dragons? More likely roaches —
     they're
          the more secure species.
     I think I'd prefer
cloning, some Kafka solution, the hard shell exterior,
            something simple inside.

The dragon grows to six feet and weighs more than
the great Jackie Gleason.
     We worship what awes us, and
          though we relegate gigantism
      to ancient Greeks and Fat Boy Burgers,
this slip of overgrown prehistory,
         these fewer than one thousand
dragons, counting

even the newt-sized newborns from the nests
of thirty-six, keeps us shuddering
      for our own specialness,
           for something
        to ward off pirates and merchants.
We are lucky, however, to believe everything wild
             tastes like chicken, except ourselves.

DRIVING L.A.

Gas collects in the tunnels I drive through
until butterflies smoke on my car grill.

The gas is transparent but can find color —
see the spill in the gutter? It's an arrangement

of atoms, a matter of excitement. Take the video
of someone who's suddenly not transparent

but beaten and angry. I am not a person of color
and my soul is less, but I too am liable

to conflagration. As I pass roadside golfers
who whack at the flames that spew up the holes

fanned by police in low copters, I see
they can't see what's collecting.

At The Castle

To say one thing when your song means another.
— Ezra Pound, *Near Perigord*

I phone Geneva, thinking Africa,
looking out the window at Italy.
The man who answers says they'll kill
each other, no one can stop them,
the UN demurs. Wine, that dark blood,
stings my nose. I take the phone

to the cliff where Pound said
nothing for ten years. You can't even
call the Sudanese, they can't agree
on a code. I say they're not starving,
the ones who are killing. You have to be
strong to rape and burn boys, boys

who sing in the dark all night,
troubadours wandering the savannah.
The wind arcs around the keep
and we both hear it. I hold
the receiver out over the battlements
and maybe the sound is someone

dying a European death,
German, Visigoth, Roman, Ice Man,
each stumbling over the bones
of the last, bones with meat
on them, bones Pound's great
grandson's dog fights for,

cut that he is. A paraglider hisses
over the pears, apples, grapes
cantilevering the slopes, taking
an exhausted loop over the spires.
Did you ever notice, I say,
how a city's most crowded cafes

offer cuisines from where the food's
most scarce? All the children under five
have starved in a province England's
size. *Well,* he says, *the big boys
who are left, what they want is guns.*

The Convoy Never Moves

Why should we hear about body bags, and deaths ... I mean, it's
not relevant. Why should I waste my beautiful mind on something
like that?

— Barbara Bush on ABC's "Good Morning America"
March 18, 2003

Flow — the guests take themselves in
and out of the utility room while
you dream them, flowing, always
backward-glancing, from the window
who would leave open with such weather
arriving with each of them? While

guests, not people you would live
with, guests not people you would
talk too much to, just *How can you*
help me? these guests are already
dead but you can't tell as they back out
of the back room with love

on their lips, but you can tell
if you look out that window
where the convoy never moves
yet tugs moan, moan again
in ecstasy, and the guests flow,
looking for other rooms, utility

being not useful to them really,
being dead already, and they move
back to where they are allowed,
into the cavities of your body while
you run in place because your mind
won't stir — the convoy never moves.

FITTING IN

In Saudi Arabia
the plane is not late, the taxi
is and all these children I have
will not fit in.
>Say they are blossoms and reasonable-sized
>and lizards from such deserts as this
>fork them — petals all over the place.

Our luggage gets chalked in swirls.
I think cloud patterns, what we're in for,
or sand. A sandbox with sides this
isn't. The plane leaves a syrup
of fuel where it can't take off,

then it does. Once on the walkway,
>the children stalk the lizards.
>The lizards have petal-shaped scales
that they eat, loosening the fit
around the mouth, tonguing the scaly
transparency inside.

>The children see this as good,
a silicon chip breakfast, smart food smarter
than pumpkin pie for hackers,
their heroes.

>They bloom while I
give out shovels
from the trunk of the taxi
and — what do you think?
>They hit each other over the head,
quarreling.
>Then they fit.

SELECTED

II. Picnic Portents

THE SEPTIC CONVERSATION

Did I mention the way water
             charts a slope across the gravel?
If not, please note. And let me suggest
              taking that south fork, for
all judgment lies with the water. That is,
shelter rises from the brink of totem,
         that is, a home on a slope is trouble.

    Take the gravel encroaching bedside.
On the south fork, which is to say,
        the one with proximity to the kitchen,
water is truth, and gravel lies. A clean fork
is what you have a shelter for,
        not the housewife standing at the sink
with its little slope, rinsing remains.

Such totem. See how one
       is atop the other — number one wife,
        number two, then children?
           It is like
             water

           water
that does not resist like gravel, the way
      gravel at the bottom of a bed gathers.
So please find water to clean whatever's
        caught in the filter. Then stop to
        hear her speak.
   She speaks.

A TERRIBLE SONATA

I

TRYST

It's not really really gothic,
the way the boy roams
the family subdivision,
grunting and "challenged,"
nor how his mother
follows him, hiding in
closets so he thinks
she's not. What romance
is there when the horror
and hero are one?

He leaves dark piles
in the foyer, bed, and back
garden to show his hate
of visitors. He can't be
bathed, except part by part
and then his manliness comes out,
furred and erect, no wand.

He does laugh, but wild,
high and hysterically.
Or perhaps it's she,
warding off his blows,
calling it love.
Who's to know — the relatives
who've moved away?
They phone to hear her sound
so tired, so tired.
But it's her child.

II

GLASS OF WATER

Drool refills it.
Fish and eels pass
his eye, banking
in the troughs
of the bubbles
he makes.

He imagines nothing:
all is present,
past and without
future: mother rhythms,
chips of quartz, oil
spots, glass.

When someone walks in,
he smiles. He doesn't
look up when the glass
is held to his lips.
He's used to drowning.

III

PARTY

The ass's tail is a challenge
even without a blindfold. All
but the smart one don't get
past turning circles. He

takes the prize, but quickly —
rising pleasure causes seizures.
Who can purse their lips?
The cake's come and the wax

of so many candles frosts it.
Such a big boy. Why doesn't
he want his toys? His hands
in his pockets, he knows what

he wants: that Mongoloid.

IV

TRAVEL

As he hoists the boy into the car,
the father's temples pound,
more in anger than exertion.

His mother pleads: *Make cow sounds,*
but he's as mute as the trees they pass.
As soon as they check in and find closets,

he starts to shout out the sounds
in his chest. Lights go on
in other rooms. *Almost human,*
says one tourist. His mother
honeys his lips to quiet him,
but he begins to thump. His father,

driving-weary, takes him for a walk,
but he wants to waltz. The hotel
Yes goes off, the moon rises,

a streak of spit, and they turn,
monster and master, together.

EURYDICE ABANDONED
IN THE CAVES OF HADES

You hire a guide. See several waterfalls,
a dock for a boat, and why not a boat?
You rock to a shore where bats rise as gulls.
Or fall. Such silence. You keep your head low,
wade black pools, one for each of the senses.
You light a cigarette, unnerved, defenseless
in the blue of that smoke. You see the roots
of trees — your sisters' hair unpinned — you see
what leads out. The sky! Then the guide rapes you,
steals your purse, and disappears. You really seethe.
Oh, god. Even Orpheus has lost it.
You can hear him through the rock, if that *Shit!*
is him shouting. You say, *Let the stones drip
their milk.* You'll sing louder, sing till you drop.

Barking Dogs

Early one Hattiesburg night,
the moon hardly dry from
the swamp bottom, the beer
already half-gone, and sleep
six hours off, a kid changes
into her tutu and tap shoes
and sings "Swanee" by the light
of the high beam.

We go wild. Even the baby,
nude as a June bug, tattoos
out a step. The kid bows
and sings the last verse
to the record cover
of her accompaniment
where sit four dogs
on blue stools in bow ties,

each a coloratura. The kid says
they go to a special school
and only eat honey. *Oh, no,*
someone uninvited volunteers.
*You just speed up a tape
and compose a scale. No dog
reads the notes bone by bone.*
The kid cries and runs off.

But we aren't going anywhere.
The mosquitoes rev up
in the few seconds she saved
from speech. What more
for entertainment — a raccoon
chained to the barbecue,
a quarrel?

Statues of Women That Are Neither Angels nor Allegory

Relinquunt Omnia Servare Rem Publicam.
— AFTER LOWELL AND WALCOTT

In Union Square her breasts are so full and stiff-
nippled surely she's nursing — or freezing.

Still she's *Love*. Three of my friends have no breasts.
What they have is five years until they get to die

like the rest of us. In the Icelandic saga,
women own as much as they can walk in a day. Every day

they walk. The Chinese say it's best to raise boys,
like the Greeks, like the couple, hands clasped,

deciding at the sonogram. Girl bones scatter the hillside
and yet — feel that man's touch, giving change,

hear the child's cry a foot away. They want.
What does Persephone say, the wheat queen's red-checked pioneer,

that compromised bitch strung out between husband and mother,
herself seasonless? The Chinese women unstrap

the toddlers from their backs to practice tai chi
in the park at dawn. At the other end, *Red Rover, Red Rover,*

little girls throw themselves over,
their arms shining with the medals of bruises.

In India, women videotape themselves working,
buckets of concrete balanced on their heads while holding

a child's hand, or weaving slats of plastic into chairs,
or stamping designs on silk over and over, then stop,

chapati for lunch, then stamp. The silk billows
fabulously around the shape of wind, the shape of life

lived after infant, after mosquitoes and fire ants
and nakedness and food. No one had ever seen them working.

Aphra Plays

Aphra Behn is not wearing all her clothes
in some part of South America nobody knows.
Everyone is polite, and not. Maybe she left off
her petticoats, her skirts look limp. She coughs.
Of course her bosom is bare. He's bats

about her, also noble and misunderstood — that's
too much culture for you. His black
skin is just skin, what with his wealth, *frisson,*
and all those bearers and banners.
The play is predominant, the manor-

house-reach. What she makes of it — not of husbands,
not even of the rights of humans richer-than-
thou, the local gentry who scheme more
than they breed — is insolence, not to bore
us. What is real is real, she says, wearing

what he wants with *Damn the insects biting.*
His type tends to the florid — strange
how everyone speaks well of him, then how chains
become him — who says that? — and someone dies,
someone like her father who fueled a nice

plantation with witty wives and loneliness and slaves
enough to drive the horses into pantaloons and full sleeves —
or play. Aphra grins at us, in disrepute
as always, sailing to England on a petticoat.

PHILOMEL

by the barbarous king
So rudely forced
— T.S. ELIOT

Aunt Phil was no fin de siècle brooched-up
elegant with one eye always on the carat,
although she almost married several goose-
bottomed men. I begin where the last
had the balls to jilt her. She'd even put down
a deposit at the engravers, spent
a mint on her teeth when he'd phoned. She pulled
the phone out. She was my mother's sister.

Letting the cost of subsequent long
long distance calls slip by and given her
now advanced age, twenty-five, we invited her
to live with us. *Poor Aunt Phil,* Mom sighed,
*she'd sooner couch-faint than admit
anybody'd hurt her.* She'd already taken
a job at a furriers. Then Dad, on his way
back from a newscast, offered to escort her.

Now Phil had Dad first, before Mom, casting us
in relative shade, but good Phil
moved away, routing this, lest we savage
the soap's adage: out of bitterness, rise
to new bitterness. Villainous as this is,
Dad stopped by anyway, offered his Mileage Plus
upgrade, saying he didn't need it, saying
all was forgiven. *Meaning?* Phil tapped.

But charmed by his new look, rewoven hair
where before large areas shone bare,
and the tacky plastic mike pinned to his lapel,
she called Mom to say she was coming, no mention

why now. Besides, it was such innocence,
the California palms cushioning takeoff,
the ever-less thirst-quenching Collins,
the overhead compartment popping open. At this point

Mom throws back the headrest on the La-Z-Boy
and I have to work out the rest myself.
Dad had not lived with us for a while. I say this
to exonerate our taste, much as parents do
with small children at table. But this was worse:
Phil and Dad retired to the plane's sole place
of liaison, and somehow in their vertical struggle,
he bit it off, that bulbed folded-over, that area

of interest, and not by accident. When she screamed,
he slipped out, jammed the door shut.
It took four men to unlock her at Newark.
She didn't turn up the day she'd promised,
but we didn't worry. She was Phil, she had her silences.
When Dad came to pick us up for the weekend,
he suggested she'd flaked off, driven crazy
by rejection. *Phil? She has plenty to choose from.*

Mom shook her head. *Just some are losers.*
Dad sighed, picked at his mike, flashed
first-run tickets. *She's just like your mother.*
Mom glared, blowing a kiss to me and my brother.
I mention him last because he meant so little
to me, being little. He was born during Dad's
re-weaving, during reconstruction, if not peacetime here.
Maybe Phil's going gay, Mom debated,

hearing nothing, or she has AIDS.
We began to worry. Then, in a final bit
of embroidery, Phil faxed Mom the truth,
each pixel in crewel design. Mom killed
my little brother and had Dad over to eat him.
This is almost literal. I mean, both ladies
split, we kids looking too much like Dad,
and it was my brother who understood

less, who drew maps of how to drive home,
who stayed in a corner for one whole year
and Dad didn't tell Mom. No, this is not
a feminist history, nor even a blowup
of the middle class. Now when Dad acts like a god
on the five o'clock news, all we can do
is turn down the sound and crow like Aunt Phil,
grappling in midair, singing our betrayal.

THE ROOT OF FATHER IS FAT

Cry uncle! but you mean Dad.
He grunts where you've socked his gut.
Post-war, he says, *men flocked to a pool*
said to dissolve fat.

But not me.
Got to have a drum in front.
Go ahead, hit me again.

The ease in the middle
lets in air between the bottom
buttons. But lean?

That's another clef
on the bacon strip. He bends over
with Atlas arms

to show you legs
upside down against a wall, to show you
veins.

Cream's good for clearing
the throat, he says. *Mmmmmmmmmmm.*
Then you can sing Sinatra.

THE ROOT OF MOTHER IS MOTH

At dusk light she slips
into acetate underclothing,
all rustling.

        Has she slept
all day? Or is that housedress
draped over the hassock warm? From her motion,
one of submission, her pale arms
                upraised, the slip sliding,
    talc issues invisibly.

Mother is faceless so far up in the dark.
Just her torso glows,
and the color around her takes on the design
of a falling leaf, grey-yellow.

      From the mirror, she draws what little light
there is inside her, and sighs.
              But she is really very young
        and will think so later.

Now nothing can claim her.
        I am quiet, all chrysalis,

THE COMMON GOOD

Imagine democracy believed in,
as common as a cold, not washing
your hands so it will spread,

the man in your bed so democratic
he's another people, watching you
insert your contacts and a horror

surfaces and he enters you
to hide it, with a lack of
tenderness you could not expect.

You see now the effect of democracy,
this man you love abstract suddenly
in his so fascinating fear of

your eye going in, and a desire
that makes you common shakes
the two of you, unbelievable.

FAMILY COURT

Though the mother does not take drugs
to keep her calm, the father is obviously
placid. The child is the train they all
climb on, even the guard. This is a saga

about motion sickness. The judge begins by
considering the mother's legs as she flips
unsteadily through truth's spectrum,
riding the narrative song of the examiner

to its logical and damaging point.
She wants to scream. The variation
possible in her replies: *Yes, but,*
are cornerstones in a edifice

of anyone's construct. Surely
the lady with the scales is scrabbling
on the floor for a lost contact.
When the judge taps his gavel,

wide as a foot, into his palm,
it's a soundless wisdom: sever
the heart and place it on a plate
for the Woodsman, uniformed and manacled.

What is the refrain?
When do they all break into dance?

THE COMPLEAT ANGLER

Sex is the boat we all board.
It's so unsteady
we can't stand up
or get ready.

Art waves from the shoreline.
Yoo-hoo!
I get harder.
I last longer.
Of course,
he can't swim.

He sends the swan
to stir the water
so what we enamor
is no longer.

He threatens:
Night will fall,
that will be all.

And, yes, the boat gets
lost offshore and drifts
and we hear his laughter
over and over
the dark water.

PUBLIC WORKS

How, in summer, a man and woman,
as in Paris, embrace under trees,
and the leaves and the grass
bend back and sweat

amends them, in a park where
the squirrels eat well, where
the bronze horse could heave off
its officer. How it is like water,

sex in summer. You cover
yourself, your leaves rippling,
the sun inside. In Calcutta,
Omdurman, even Paris, the bent

grass curls and dies and birds
take it away until slums root,
the trees bare in smooth hard lust.
Touching a man there as if no one

but the exiles espaliered
to the bare walls watch,
just the occasional touch. How,
at the far end, another bronze

beckons, her robes folded over
children and jugs of water,
and Haitians pass her by, hands clasped,
walking home into

the dark. How the roundness
of their faces shines as leaves, not money.
How, when the general dismounts,
swords fall from the arches,

speeches sigh from the trees,
and his first words to her
are what's carved in
by the ghostlike, love-struck loiterers.

THE SIXTIES

Every age, like every human body,

has its own distemper.

— EMERSON

Were we the only ones swimming nude
                under the overpass?

                        Every interchange
in river country engorged you,
triggered musk so thick our clothes
                stuck.

                        And afterward,
sunning on the car hood, if we spoke
                of having children, it was pure praise,
the organs smacking after,

                                not premonition.

Were all those other stops
                at hilltops with overlooks and bushes,
                at roadside parks with hidden tables,
                at empty barns scoured by rats,
                                lanolin-sweet, fertile,

        just the produce
of an era, so many of us solving

                                sex over and over,
its sunset flushed

the whole country? Or if I now
                park the child-thick car
                        and fight my way into some
mosquito-whining copse,
                will I still find a couple?

DOWNHILL ROMANCE

Jammed cock to buttock
we slice through the snow
screaming: *no moon, no moon.*
The gully below blazes with a lighter,
then a cigarette's star.

Just short of its smoke, his legs
cascade into a drift like salt
into the street. I land on
barbed wire and bare rock.
The stopping is terribly silent.

As I rise on my elbows, she drops
her butt into the snow and laughs.
I help drag the sled around her
while she shouts: *Was it fast?*
Once on top, you empty your boots.

Never do you touch me. Even when
crashing is imminent, you don't grab
at my breasts. While I warm up,
your hood joins hers for kisses.
Again she'll wait this one out.

Stung with scrub, we plough
into a bag of marshmallows and then
walk home, following someone's
long strides in the snow, like
spacemen in all our clothes.

I shiver as new flakes spin up
into the streetlight. When you put
your hands into her pockets
and talk of the moon's craters,
I ask: *How many could one hold?*

SAILING EXCURSION

Blue and white tiles surround
our hearth, as Dutch an embellishment
as the boats seeming to glide
over the land, the land
invented only to separate one boat
in the canals from another.

In the foreground, we gather at breakfast
in Breughel's jerseys of brown and perhaps
a scarlet shoe, our porridge
doused in milk from a cow so laden
her teats are wooden to our

thieving touch. In this gold light
we smoke, kiss, and say all relgion
is psychology. Then the wind blows us
back to the water maze, so like life
in that we can't turn back. The trees
are few, the horizon close as a hand yet

big with clouds roiled in argument.
Dusk has a smokey wick, as if more
time is allotted us, prisoners
of a holiday. Where are we going?
We are too young to bother with anything
other than pleasure: Bach draws

the sails. Yet we do dock, as silver
in the fresh moon as foreign money
and with awe: those we'd left behind
to try sex lit candles all along the shore,
creating a hopelessly dangerous tableau,
like love, its proscribed country.

ALL ABERRATION

A steak smell invades my path
but a woman walks by with lilacs
and cancels it. *Spring*, my son
says from his stroller, or maybe
sing — I'm too proud to hear less.

We pass parks and parking lots
where in this season only
the very young don't look foolish
in love. Old men behind their trucks
with stumped women, bald and lolling
in embrace — they're aberration.

It's all aberration, my palmist
states, sorting one flame from another,
I believe him. Last year my friend
was murdered, bludgeoned
by his wife's lover, his own best friend.

Yet it's the age of sudden death:
at thirty, life's less an accumulation
than a situation you've made
for yourself. The stroller's
losing a wheel, but with a little wire
I make it. Then thirty flights up,

rain on every story and the sitter
extending her arms. My son whimpers.
Even in the best of families.
Another woman drops off her brood.
so like lizards the way their heads turn.

The elevator releases me,
allows my womb to snap
for its contents. Sex is next.
I say, *You're too rich,*
your fingers move over my hands

like fence shadows over a train,
nothing's been necessary
to you since the Armada.
And so, he's too tired.
I collect my son and start
for home. The rain has flattened

the tulips on the median,
petals splash the dark ground.
As I cross the last street,
a man in a taxi whistles,
taking the carriage as a sign
I once did desire, and more.

SONNET

Three bursts of birds clear the roof.
How many? I ache to add everything.
I'm on my third drink, *mon amour,*
you're that late. Yesterday's
story of how wolves surrounded
the car and how you tossed the baby
out to scatter them was

fine but what about the frozen
raccoon I found behind the ice cubes?
We're all sick and exhausted.
It's not your slim red car glimpsed
between the trees that I long for.
It's the running over, the forward
and reverse, the nest from the tree.

SUSURRUS OF SHEETS, GOODBYE

He leans across his arm, peeks
at her hose-crotch bed-height,
her breasts doubling over.
It's no artist's pose, feet in a basin,
pin shivers in pointillesque,
but the hair she holds off her neck
sends heat into him. Otherwise,

color and motion, the day's
global positioning ratchets
into place with a purse click.
Sweet, she says into the near dark.
She could mean the sudden breeze
except he catches her hand
against his rough cheek.

OCTOPUS

After cueing, he stretches TV-wall-mount height,
runs a couple of Fahrenheit-
hot-hormoned, tricep-bicep-and-vein-bulging
arms your ass-wise, while in
full *sostenuto,* lays out each syllable
of your name. Then all his pockets fill.

You eye the beer he bought you,
even lean in to watch him voodoo
the geometry, the physics, the smack
of cue-to-green, fingers sliding off-rack,
the sudden weight of his thumbs hooked
to your jean belt, his cigarette sucked

so his *Hi* heats your ear, the way his hand
arcs around to powder the tip damned,
destined to drop to your nipple,
waist, crotch as if will
is nothing you can accuse him of, glancing
shark-like at a green ball, the scene

so early on your rights-radar you sip
at the beer, you lean back to gossip
with the ham-thighed matron handing out nuts
(his?) who might be married to him. *Buttercup?*
he calls her, *Hit me again.* And for once
she does, educationally, a straight-on punch.

AUBADE

Sinews here and there,
his legs twined at desk
and all of him bare,

mousing around, *click,*
so the child won't wake.
Sinews, his sex thick

but laptopped, glasses
found then lost then
a child flushes

and my hands on him
count only as clothes,
as information.

Sinews, I say *sotto voce,*
and he smiles into
his screen. At me?

DUMB HUSBAND

As the right brain twines around the left
and forgets it
        so
                Sepulveda takes several turns
     and we lose the thread of it,
our adult exchange, for once not money-based
   or in the liturgy of children,
      whatever it was, lost at
          the first unfamiliar interchange.

Beaches, palms, 7-11, a corridor
  of thick brick stoops,
     the level is now Yes or No
and a nervous stomping on the gas
                 pedal.

      I drive. There are worlds to miss
    if you're always right,
the only argument for travel,
   true adventure. Look at it this way.

      You look at it this way.
A semi does not. Its lower tones
    reach our children's bones and a sorrow
links us all, the crabby baby,
     the boy pillowed in comics,
                me
turning off
    then on again.

    You rattle the map
       with a flair for forgiveness
saying, *It's true,*
     I never talk to you.

PINK

In China I remembered you only once:
the restaurant's speciality, chosen
from a braid of live varieties,
spiraled to the floor while the waiter
flayed it with a knife flicked

from his wrist. The snake made your initial
over and over the black tile.
What pain! *Love's all touch*
was the ideogram it made as it crossed
the hot stones to the table.

MARRIAGE BOAT

Gulls ogle and swoop those in the boat,
even those with children, even those

with eyes fixed as figureheads.
Flesh! Flesh! the birds scream.

Rope is not the operative word here
but line, as sex alone suggests

sibilant potential, not love.
At any time the stern could disappear

back to where it came from,
the clouds herding their foam away

from reflection. Yet it seems, on clear days
when no one's crying, it seems

as if the boat bears both ocean and sky,
and the bodies fly, hiked so far out.

KITTENS

Though the wheat fuzz tickles her knee scabs,
her face is stern as she positions the thermos
like a bayonet. Her mission is to deliver

the lemonade. The fields all around outshine
her hair that must be washed by Wednesday,
scalloped into French braids by her clumsy

mother who now fishes an ice sliver
from inside her dress front. As the child
swims into the grain, the mother pleats

her brow: the kittens caught in the backwater
now float and must be strained and burnt
or buried. She smoothes on rubber gloves,

her movement perpendicular to the scythe
the machine far off has not put down, the blade
over the father and the open thermos.

Hares, he says. He hates to talk.
Dun and gray speckled, like all things wild,
they squirm in a crescent of uncut wheat.

The girl puts them to her, their newborn forms
writhing against her plum-sized womb,
and the fields bend glossily as she makes

her return. *You're cruel to keep them,*
shouts her mother, hair singed, the yard stinking
and ash sticking to the cherry tree leaves.

Hiding, the girl falls to sleep in the warm barn
under a harness. The bunnies, dazed, nearly green
in the dark, hop out of their tomato flat

and the cat who has been watching streaks for them.

BRIDGE, MOTHER

Mother burns on the other side of the bridge.
Mother burns the bridge and is safe on the other side.
Mother is not on the bridge when it burns.
When Mother says burn, the bridge burns.
We can't get to the other side,
the bridge is burning.

Mother is the bridge that we burn.
She is how we get to the other side.
We can't burn the bridge without her.
Mother burns and we burn, bridge or no bridge.
She is the other side.
Nothing burns the bridge, and then it burns.

PICNIC PORTENTS

Spiders live in all the park cupolas,
                                                    the joints
                        she ties the balloons to.

                                See the fake steer roping,
the wire horns and the stiff rope? It's this hollering that exhausts,
                not the horseshoes.

                                Fishing for forks, she says,
When my husband dies then I'll know.
                                Another woman holds up a finger.
Who says sex
                        and death for seventy?
Jeopardy, says the next.

While parachuting down,
he pinned on stripes and medals — a corporal's —
                so they would treat him better. That one, over there —

All but one woman turn.

                        It was in the mayo. Thirteen out of forty,
                two infants. You'd think they would have choked
on the potato.

Danae puts the box with the boy and herself in
out
                past the boat launch.

SEX AND CLASS AND RACE

Books say parents
didn't mourn their children

in previous centuries, that
nose-wipes and infants

died as edelweiss on a granite face,
so much sex in excess.

But at the very least, the poor
had their need for labor.

Perhaps the rich left children
to wolves or footmen,

perhaps they saw a child
as a purse divided.

Perhaps.

But even their women ran
into the snow, not to return,

or cut something again and again
so it wouldn't mend.

Yet people do forget.
Even I forget,

blind in the dark passage,
bent as the Victorian foliage

that screens me from them,
so sepia-dirty in their sullen

photos they might be another race
if color is what it takes

to dodge such sorrow.

HOW TO SIMPLIFY FRACTIONS

Put the big one
over the small one
and what do you get?
Don't tell.
He was a big man
and the first time
the boy cried.

Sometimes the wounded
use their scars.
Pull up the small one's
sleeves now, see all
the lines,
fine white
at the wrist,
where the answer goes.

DICK IS DEAD

1930-2002

Dick is dead.
Pedophelia has lost its head.
Long live the town instead.

Photo and radio pro,
he issued invites and bon mots
to wives waiting by the telephone

while bedside,
awash in *au jus,* kids cried.
He didn't catch AIDS.

He did
the annual ski trip
with skinny dips.

No-Knock Dick,
he invaded our house with lilacs
or booze or new paint chips.

Only one
of my brothers broke down.
We are glad Dick is gone.

Xmas House

Could I plunge my ballpoint into
your throat the moment you purple —
   even then? Make a gaping hole
for air where the syllable catches? If we
     invented whipped cream
and its canister to deplete the ozoned air,
   that suicidal turn, what about
a gingerbread beam to block it?

   You breathe gingerly, Heimlich-bruised,
   and the boy under the tree
   points the canister down his throat
and misses, the spray
    making a kind of white beard.
It's for him you are saved,
    and the house. I grab

the one throwing himself over the edge
   of the carriage, who does an *entrechat*
being lifted, whose syllable is *la*
   after forced feeding.
As the dog takes food pellet by pellet
   to the carpet and swallows,
    we forget how brave the baby is.

ROCK POLISHER

A worm
inside this one, he says.

Over and over he grinds it,
an unclear oval of brown,

        its edges rough and grit.
The polisher echoes with violence.

Hollow maybe, he says.
Except for the worm.

        Among the rubies

it lies, among smooth gravel.
We think dragon
                but he means

        anger. What else do boys
conquer?

Held to the light so,
and away,
        the tail flicks.

As the Birds

I felt very poor that year,
sleeping by the car, under stars,
my child and the lover,
each in their own furrow,
the dirt humped like graves,
and mornings, wetting the ash
in my mouth and swallowing it,
the price of consciousness.
We were not bums but bathed daily

in a sluice or by some weedy cottonwood
and we never went hungry or I'd still
hear the child calling out in the night,
desperate as a predator. Still,
we had no home, no work to return to.
The trees thickened to forest or
balded to desert while why we drove
became as absurd as those gobbed bloodied gnats
spread on the windshield.

But when the child sang, we sang.
And when he cried, we sang.
No radio told us of tornadoes
nor of what else we'd find (sleep,
food, friends) and when the child
napped on the sticky vinyl, we looked
in this same thicket for love,
as if it had been left for us alone,
under the low leaves.

Once we ducked into an empty farmhouse,
its linoleum buckling with dog's pee,
and found the watchdog himself where
the mice had cleaned him. We didn't
pass by to plump the beds. We'd

forgotten about beds anyway,
and the child hadn't known them,
just breast, just the soft hollow
of my arm, so we stayed on the porch
and the rain kept the dark after dawn.

PLUG

The instruments of life on video:
the pulse, breath, brain will shrink
to a single pop of light whenever I say.

I said test him when at three he read
Babar. He hid under my skirt, mum so long
the man with the pointed beard gave up.

He's warm, Miss, isn't he? His color's
good? Never mind. I have an hour to decide.
But his turnip head, what the doctors said.

Each night he read the same three books
and I went right to sleep. As parents do,
I peeked to check his chest, its rise

and fall with regularity. That the room
should go quiet is unendurable. Like a god
I decree others take what parts he has and live.

Like eggs his organs leave.

THE NEEDLE WITH BOTH HANDS

Always fatal, Tay-Sachs disease affects
only Eastern European children.
FOR R.N.B.

Over the waves of his chest,
you watch the sun go up, again. How
accidentally the birds cross it!
How seemingly accidental.

What random choices led you
to him — your darling
from the same steppes
as Zhivago's, and your own.

Then he's dressed, and you're almost.
Leaning over, he pulls your slip up
to put his hand over that fat part of you,
where swims the swimmer. Enter

              Tay and Sachs,

two men good at identifying
     a certain kind of certain death
          due to a certain mix of genes
               of children with certain parents.

Today you go to determine your chances,
rather, its chances,
all euphemism unable to cover
the chance red spot on the growing retina.

After your doctor has his way,
you can see on the screen
the little swimmer trying to escape,
holding the needle with both hands,
                  just reflex.

                    The verdict
takes time to swell and ripen.
The doctor offers his only balm, a curse:
knowledge without antidote. All you know

is that the immortals throw no bones,
that you inherit nothing
but genes and bravery, both faltering.
You trot back to work

and your new belly swirls with
the fetal pig you took the eyes from,
grade ten. To market, to market.
You pull your goddamn shrinking coat

around you. Nothing like
the stir of life that has no chance.
You shrug. It's only the size of your finger,
you don't care —

                    But knowing at the end
of ten hours' pitched screaming,
your insides reversing, you get
                              nothing —

          What goes where with death?
You know all about life.
You majored in biology, pirouetted
through the wedding night.

Does it make sounds yet?
Choose happiness but accept the truth:
the child might die, you tell your husband.
                                        Suffer and die.

In the three-week wait you type,
and each hammer moves the days along.
Waiting, every word from everyone hurts,
every *Good day,*

                    careless or concerned,
every word. The only sympathy you want
is the same cruelty shared, all else
grates. Inside, it spins — in fear?

What you must swallow
is the sugar cube of your continuing,
the inescapable desire to pee
that stirs you mornings, hours before dawn.

But if,
          at the end of these weeks of waiting,
the white-masked priests come back bearing
no news, which is their best,

you will have brushed off Death,
rimed him bright and acceptable
                              and seen it slant.
Either way.

              That is, what happens
doesn't matter. You eat.
You lie down. The sun shrinks.
          The daily din you're thankful for

rescinds its paper currency that nothing backs up.
        Your husband puts on a pot to boil, and another.
He can't feel it inside, though he's eaten the same
sour apple, bearing half the genes,

those underclothes, the bra, the brief
of the body. You are dumb
before his helplessness. The cord to belly to cord
will not be broken,

ripped untimely as it may be.
Mama has happened
                and the rocking horse of your heart
heaves on.

SLAVE CHILDREN

Qui tacet consentit.
HE WHO IS SILENT AGREES.

Something Latin here for
twelve hour days that says no play
but the fingers' equal
the tiny stitches of a bargain.

A soccer ball kicked — I'm not saying
it isn't my skin too. With days
for them a series of nights,
the idea of choice, just the idea —

not the way getting lunch early seems lucky —
is *Surprise!* They kill or work
as commerce requires,
necessity a little bracelet of sound.

GONE WAVE

The wet sand, scoured, shows
plant-green hair I could swim through
but not save.

I could dream this
as prophecy. I could forget.

         I suction
my sand-heavy suit
off the surf floor.

The next wave,
lens-clear, holds
the boy up in more
light than wave,

each eyelash
separate, the arm-bend
not right.

I spit foam, press water
with my hands.

He rises again,
just about to be born, to be borne —
Mother —

now and no more.
The last wave a looking away
in so much water.

SELECTED

III. DEATH STAYED

THE HIGH COST OF PRINCIPLE

Shadowed by a dog,
        the infinite dog, mirror of all
in all the leaves,
            I bark faithfully
because we are one
            and the cherry pie offering
that glistens in the snow,
        organs he's left after the kill,
the jays disagree on.
                    Still I walk
            into where the birds aren't,

with the principle wagging the dog
        in my forebrain. If there were
no dog, says the dog, circling,
        making a kind of floe
            with his prints cutting through,
the fruits would be gathered this day
        same as the next. Thus
            I offer my neck.

SISTER LOVE

I'm underground and there's a drip.
It could be calcium, it could be sorrow.
The dark, though, suggests self-pity.
Who's breathing?
                    My brother on his blue satin.

It's as if all my life I waited
and the wait killed him. Here, it's underground
                    and cold and

I'm driving and mist breaks around me
so I have *something to show,*
meaning my body. It's not
that I put on those rubber gloves
backwards, Cocteau's *Orphée,*

or even get out of the car —
                    fire explodes in the slick
                    as I pass.

Surely he puts on his gloves
and goes to work, as clumsy as ever.

The way sugar sets hunger is enough
to imagine what sets death. Imagine
the cave alive, lava surging,
an excited sorrow
                    because I said so.

NIGHT SAIL

A rare cloud covering the whole
of the moon, or the dog on its hindlegs, howling?
            Who cares — I'm awake, and alone. It's so quiet

the dream is the water at the windowsill
            and the darkness that plaits it,
                        the hair of Greek women,
                                    thick, black, curled
                        with connotation, the usual wailing.

            I fear, and the accursed windchimes
barely chime.
                        I'm even inclined to cry. How easily
the bay would take its rearing prey, one black wind
            snapping the mast —
                        you'd left at nine.

            The buoys strain, a tinkling
                        that gives up nothing. If the earth's round,
my love's still here, somewhere.
                                    So I hear what I want,
i.e., the widow's walk wasn't put up
            for solace. But nothing's there,
                        a disquieting stillness in the air.
            I find the door,
                  my nude length gliding out like milkweed
                        or any other blossom
                                    gone unheeded.

            Each plank in the yacht club's boardwalk
receives me musically.
                        I can't fuss.
            If some drunk
                        boatsman should roll over and see —

It is cold, and getting colder but I don't retreat.
I stare at the lapping water, its landlocked
            gibberish. It's the wind I'm after,
its overture: *return, return, return.*
        If only some triangle
                would blot out the stars,

                            or a dusting of oars ...

THE DOG IN THE WALL

They said that's where Lulu
went, that was the smell. Not
rats.

Fifty years go by. They say
Yes, they don't change their story,
it's true.

A low cement-block fence around
the house, a collie dog bark,
four kids.

Not collie but collie dog, Howdy
as in Doody, *The Stooges* on someone else's
TV.

It barked less than we kids
howled, all of us waiting to move in,
the dog's tail

in our faces. No room for a big dead dog,
our first built house,
2 by 4s

at most, no crawlspace. Propitiatory,
an offering to a worksite in winter,
a shovel

to the head? They laugh.
We never saw the dog again,
the old house

too far to run back to, our scent long gone,
the busy roads with their big cars,
the pawing,

clawing against the sheetrock
my ear touches. Squirrels? The panting.
The whine.

MY MATURE STYLE

I light matches endlessly.
Paris burns!
The Eiffel Tower shoots blue gas!
The lighter I find in my pocket,

cold metal on a blue bruise,
ignites the biggest fires.
I get dogs and cats running,
I get affirmation in black.

My mother's heart keeps on burning.
Mark the left ventricle her favorite,
its system so silent and skilled,
its blue the blues of exchange.

CYCLES

Without a moon or light,
my bike floats, all balance.

I open my mouth, *O sole mio*
but my voice could be the road,
dippy and suddenly ending.

A friend bikes out of the black.
I heard you and I hurried.

I wobble, startled, but my wheels
whine forward. We can't even see
the grass brushing our calves.

Soon the road narrows
and a creek cuts one side,

you can hear water
on its own path, and surely
there's a ditch — surely.

We bike in file, hunched,
bearing the dark until

a car comes up behind us,
lights off. We pedal hard, harder.
The car comes on anyway,

it is coming. Before its grille heat
signals where,

there's a terrible crash,
the late pop
of an airbag, there's the ditch

and the grass, we weave and —
there's no sound after,

just a metal something
rolling.
We kickstand our bikes.

No *O my god*. Just *What?*
What? my friend, gasping.

We run back.
If we search for the driver apart,
we're lost, but together,

we're doubly blind.
We touch and touch.

The sharp grass, the flitter of insects,
the uneven earth underfoot —
we want not to find

anything. But Death says
we must, both of us,

and the road
we followed, the road
the car left,

will disappear.

INVENTOR

The jay streaks through the lilacs
                  in color clash.
I note down: Invent
             outdoor birdswing
                              so birds drunk
on berries fall off in plaid
             in front of my window.
                                    I file it. After all,

the pussy willow's barely tufted —
                             I have time.
          At the drain, lifting its feet,
               a Modigliani bird — another invention?
The brook agrees
               so brookishly, gulping at runoff
                    like a bear in spring,
            like my husband. He didn't trust my patents:

               the squirrel-free gutter chain
                    the collapsing arthritic's cane
            a lever for pulling old stumps
                     in heavy rain.

But every act harbors a corresponding gadget.

                    It is that way with God:
adjusting the acorn, locking the tree.
          With the womb, He was clearly Italianate,
the bulbous lines, the excess.
          I often think of Him
               humming Beatles songs like me, over
                   six Mason jars of pickling —
my offspring?
          The dog laughs. You heard it:
a choke, then black gums, a frothing irony.

He's all wet from rescuing bones
        from the brook. He drops them in,
                        then goes in after.
The brook's rising with bones and I'm afraid
the electricity will fail. Will the dog

                save me with his laughing?
        Guess what this invention's for:
the automatic rosebush waterer,
        hooked to the sun and this wheel,
in perpetuity. Once a pirate working
on my outboard told me: better sand
        trickling in the hourglass than a shifting dune.
                        Even the Sudanese
plant borders of aloe against the drifts.
        But I like the look of roses.

        Oh, that's the husband at the door, scratching.
Nights his furry self stands naked
        before me, until the dog
removes his stuffing.
                O bear! Only by opening
        the blinds do I see he's bleeding.
        It's him, not me, aching
                with overdue maternity.
        A simple drawerful of cobwebs
kept for emergency does for him,
        self-sticking,

        then together we apprise
                the chimney,
holding hands and chatting about the soot stains.
        That was in winter before he died, the deft
                air stealing all we were speaking.

                                    Yesterday
              a patent came for my speech retrieval unit,
           an unusual event, even for me, because
                 the government usually can't get
past the drawings. And these were intricate:
              I had the duck by the neck, her feet
                    in food coloring, each step
           inked in. It all made sense — listen
to the ducks now. And just in time for the aspect —
                 ghosts are aspects, aren't they?
           Of all but speech I have memory,
                          that one sense shy of mimicry.

              In the spring, now, in fact,
I take the blackfly larvae off rocks
                                in the rapids.
              On toast, pre-maggot, the very eggs
                    of mortality, eating them I figure
           I can lure Death itself, a raccoon
washing and washing in the dark,
                    and from there, patent the trap.
           I'll be rich if it works.
                 Works, go the frogs, *works, works.*

124

PICNIC

The birdcalls are louder than Route 9 traffic,
all lung, but you can't find them,
staring at the bottom rungs of a dead pine,
at the deciduous aching with blossom.
The calls may as well be friction over holes
in space, or all legend, the bewitched
fussing in the boughs for attention.
You deflect the ants from your path,
thinking how one could brush away success
like a harmless nuisance. And with your
friends — you tackle the main hill with
a twig — your success would linger, a sour dishrag,
the job over. In double dactyls now,
the birds, and an ant successfully
drags a chestnut. You're stuck

in the *Why bother?* Like fertilizer or
fairy dust, hope gets tracked across
the cleaned-up floor. All those fabulous
bird tales, vulture versus hawk, promote this.
You sit on a hollow log that sinks in decay.
Listen, what about enchantment? A red fox
matching last fall's foliage, pads by, then
caught by the smell of you, turns its head.
You both want to run but not together. You sing
My Old Kentucky Home low so he stops.
If he were shot, the killer would think
he was doing you a favor. Last year success
was superconductivity, it happened in space
where no one lived. The birds go quiet.
You hug the anomalous sandwich.

THE RULE OF K

Give someone a name beginning with K if you want a hero.
— NEIL SIMON

In the dead body:
        my brother, doppelganger.
Look over
my shoulder:
                he too was paranoid.
                        But what's
natural cause at forty?

        At night he'd open
the first volume and read:
Aardvark, earth pig, 3½ feet long,
        then read to K,
                then sleep.

        K's the vitamin
they give you if you bleed.
                I had K in Africa,
miscarrying like a pig,
        some other lady
dead without it,
                the double.

        What divides me from him —
eleven months
eighteen days —
will never close.

        But who was that fat Karen
after his money and why

did he keep a crippled cat
              he couldn't catch?

      The sound of K multiplies –
Christ, another paranoid,
           with a name you can hear
from every pew, was born again
in the month he died.

                  I need a hero.
Hear the cat
           he couldn't catch,
crying for liverwurst?
What's worse than liverwurst?

        My brother ate it
to prove he wasn't me.
Now, surely, he's not.

THE RANCHHAND'S DAUGHTER

I

Not even the Indians who worshiped land
could abide this barrenness. They shunned it,
left bears' bones at its spent perimeter.
Blasting the presidents' faces in made
for a helluva slide, tourists, exits
lined with arches framing Ozymandian
reaches. When herds die in these ravines, no one
notices until spring when snowmobiles
whine, flipping over the drifts, landing
upright. And if sometimes stories circulate
about big spreads and the ranchhand's daughter,
it's only the Badlands seeking substance.
With its goddess rising from a shell sunk
in the ooze of lost natural gas, with flames
obviously next, like scarves when the wind
whips up, which it always does, the land swims
against the sun, against the unending
anonymous roll of the hills, perfect
for the innocent goddess, the hulking
he-god, the forever-kneeling supplicant.

II

Junco, meadowlark, warbler, hawk burst up
out of the sagebrush like a backshuffled
card deck as she drove forward with nothing
for a road. She didn't know any better, the web
of interstate thinned forty miles beyond
their three sections and the county seldom
fixed washouts. Her Chevy pickup took drops
the way a horse would, solemn and picky.
Right where the Lazy Y creekbed lent view
to the gully, canyon really, the walls ran
red yellow blue green welts along the side.
Although beauty burst from her at eighteen,
she knew best the grimy eyeletted moon
hanging a foot out of the trash dump.
Her wheels shivvied rock, then she tried to turn,
a couple of steers looked up, bothered, and
the salt lick in the back shifted so far
her front wheels left the ground, turning over.
To that, the radio popped on, the steers
drummed off, and all the birds in a mile hid.

III

Blair wasn't much of a nurse. He cranked up
the heat, served spaghetti out of a can,
and killed flies. She didn't die. Doc Parks,
the vet, set the bones. He happened to see
the fire. *Keep ice on her. You got ice?* Blair
frowned *Yes,* and the ranch hand fetched it. *You should
haul her out to the hospital despite
the trouble with her mother.* Blair left the room.
Doc Parks put a vial on the old bureau.
Ernie — the hand was back — *These are for horses.*
Tell Blair to half them before he feeds her.
And if she gets a fever, send for me.

She fevered. Blair took his car into town
and got drunk. She was in the talking sweats
when Ernie found her and made compresses
soaked in coffee. Didn't have no tea. After
he put out the feed, he sat by her bed
reading horoscopes from last week's paper.
Then, dreaming, there was her mother, alive,
sawhorse legs, double belly, cigarette
breath from smoking them up so fast she had
to go to town and going finally
out to the hospital cemetery
where for some reason a red cactus grew up
that never had to be watered. He woke.

IV

Once in a while Blair'll stop at the soddie.
The vetch is so high there you almost can't
get inside but you know when you're in it —
it's chilly and the wind stops. This last time
he could still hear the neighbor twenty miles
off in his spray plane. He shivered. The cold
made him feel in hell. Funny, being cold,
the window hole hot to the floor with light
poured on it. I'd like to start fresh, he thought,
but that would be fresh like fish, eyes clouded,
gills stinking, a smell for something living
too far away. I'd like to start —
It isn't for nothing I have her come
to me. They say the drop of a donkey
and a mule is worthless. I say it goes
back to the mare. I want her mother, over
and over. All I have is need shaking
in my hands, a corner that I bite from,

backed into. Oh, wife. He spotted the fake bronze
plaque the Duchess County Historical
Society put up saying this was
Jesse James' hideout when he laid low
disguised as a woman. Blair always felt
embarrassed by it. Before she was gone,
his wife said, *You missed your time. You should
have a real gun, fine boots, and luck at cards.*
He punched the two-foot-thick wall but didn't
do much else. There's the mark, a clod short that side,
under the picture of the Virgin. Hey,
that's who it is. I'll be. The dark litho
fluttered. With one broad filthy finger he
smoothed it, then stood there in a daze, sensing
worship wouldn't matter, having little
to do with either him or his daughter.

V

Only a slight rolling, the sand bedspread
rumpled, the chenille tufts pockets of sage
so spicy burnt that the ash had a taste.
Only a slight rolling generally,
the gully full of skulls, the sky bending
over a big blue backache. She's mended,
the horizon so bright under her blind,
pulling it down was an escape. Only
on Sundays did they do no work and she hid.
Blair — why should she call him father? — stayed
waiting alone until he shouted for her.
She ran off to the trap room once, in amongst
the spiked metal that smelled of rust and blood.
But he came for her. The hired hand played pool
just yards away in his bunkhouse or sat
in his naugahyde recliner fixing
harness or polishing his pneumatic bow
and arrow. From his picture window
(the house being trailered from Ovid) lay
her car, still twisted. He would work on it,
but not Sundays he told her, he didn't like
being so close to the house then, though why
he never said, a dog's caution, maybe.

VI

Double eight ball over, sun in clover,
you're my lover or some such palaver
on the radio. The girl came running,
the screen door banging over and over,
running as best she could with one leg still
screwed up out to the trap room which was strange,
given how much she hated that skinning
business, then Blair, coming after, but
insistent, calling as if he really
really wanted to find her. Blair's wife
used to say, *Ernie, you're gonna get curtains*
if I have to use my old half slips. Of course
real long ago. He turned from the window.
On the arm of his recliner he'd found
the girl's name scratched in, just yesterday he'd
seen it, watching TV, the rest of him
sleeping. Colt-legged she was when he'd come,
grizzled from too long on a road crew. When
she turned sixteen, and her father refused
to pay money to bus her to high school,
he'd felt sorry. He'd found a coyote cub
and brought it in a box to her, leaving
it alongside the porch. But Blair found it,
slit its throat before she saw it. *Good work,*
Blair'd praised him, *Got to get at them young.*
Ernie'd nodded, took off the pelt, stuffed it
into a wall crack in his cold front room.

And she stumbled out sobbing.

VII

Mother, I lost the doll you once twisted
out of cornsilk for me. It was better
than Barbie. I still watch all the programs
you used to, and iron too. The sand cranes
still come in the spring, so like the flapping birds
you made from newspaper, and storks too. Storks.
I was nine when you died, no baby but
not yet grown. You didn't say much except
that TV told some real bad fairytales.
We were sad about you together, Mom,
then just I was sad. But you often teased
Ernie, Dad says it, so I must come out
of a line of this type lady who likes
it. I'm sorry but I don't though. I like
catkins on my cheeks better, or nothing.
Yesterday I couldn't come visit you
because he hadn't yet. I love the square
with your name written in so the warblers can
pick at the June bugs that stray over,
and all the wind hollering down the slope
to where there's a real road and a place for
signs. I'm glad you're in the hospital lot
even if Dad says it's for bad women.

VIII

Mallards dive into the bright green custard.
Frogs lay their eggs in it, so thick they hatch
airborne, and none escape the hungry ducks.
So few cows commence to drink from this spring
that the grass at its edges is a downy
green, a velveteen. She smoothes her hand
across it, expecting a stain. She's
never been here before, though she's driven
or walked far into her father's land. Slow
as a miracle asked for, the sun crops
a lone tree and the effort of the day
touches itself. She punches on the car
lights, holding the mirage before her like
Jell-o over an oven, or moments
of television, then she turns toward stars
high enough in the horizon that they're
not fake and, keeping far from the dead cow
with calf mostly eaten, she drives straight home.

IX

The horizon was what barred her. If she
put her hand up, she could grab it, if she
drove, there wasn't any way to get there.
School proved to be torture, a one-room-rule,
every kid as badassed as the bus that
brought them, and her, the farthest, five a.m.,
first stop, seven return, the last hour just
her and fat Mrs. Finstrom, the driver/
substitute who admired the cornsilk doll
she kept inside her jacket, who once gave her
a pair of pantyhose and then died of
insulin shock, or, some of the bad kids
said, of overeating. No one came home
with her to play — but this was normal, she
didn't miss what she'd never had. Her breasts
budded, her majority came, eased in
by classmates pointing to the brown skirt spot,
singing out *Apple butter, Apple butter.*

When she started to fatten she ate less.
She unbuttoned her jeans, held them on with
rope, wore her blouses loose. Ernie caught her
saddling up, her scrawny arms high, her blouse
parting. Even he, motherless, with no
sisters, and a bachelor, could see the foal
coming. *That's something,* he said. *Your dad know?*
She hid her eyes. *No? You got to tell him.*
He dragged her off the horse by her jean loops.
Who was it, he roared halfway to the house,
Leonard? A half-breed selling satellite
dishes had come twice because she liked to
look at the pictures: aborigines
in Australia, spacemen in construction,

the dish a sort of hollyhock. Her dad
was with a sick cow both times so Ernie,
well, he sat and looked at the pictures too,
the first time, then couldn't take the repeat.
She shook her head while he shook her, then cowered:
He knows.

        He let go her arm.

                Pardon me.

X

For three months Ernie kicked silence around
like an old cow flop. He didn't move fast,
polished up his one bareback trophy and
the floor clean enough to eat on. She swelled
like a two-door with a calf in the back.
Counting backward, Ernie ascertained that
Leonard was clear out of the county that
time, and pitied her. Then in cold December,
the wind unforgiving, the cows bawling
in the feedlot, when changing the oil
in the pickup took forever, Ernie went
out to check on the cows. The heifers stood
on their heaped-up silage and, grape-eyed, stretched
their necks, bitterly ululant. Because
the cow-scratcher flapped loose from the barbed wire?
No, the trough under the windmill was why —
Blair face down in it like he was looking
at the bottom, and the extension plugged
to the floodlights sizzling next to his head.
Ernie said, *You wash up first.* She had his shirt
on over her ripped-up nightie, and Blair
was nude. *I don't know nothing.* Ernie shook
himself, climbed the fence, let the cows loose.

XI

She delivered that day. Twisting his lips
the way he did when pulling calves, he watched.
The girl got wild and sobbing but didn't
beg for no one, not mother, and no man,
and cursed its sex as it delivered. *Let it
strangle.* But Ernie cut the cord and laid
the baby by her. *Now,* he said, *we need
relief.* He dialed up emergency, then
swept the house. She couldn't leave. She tried, trailing
afterbirth like a cat.
                                      *Sometimes they turn
themselves in, but Ernie? Really?* Sheriff
Potts waived bail and even the unit loaned
from the capitol couldn't do much more
than fingerprint him again. Neither of them
had an alibi. Who could stand as witness —
coyotes, cruising the rock-flecked range? She nursed
the baby through the inquest and wasn't
allowed to testify. Innocence sucked
in the silence. Perplexed, the judge deemed it
an accident, a man combing his hair,
nude, in winter, and a loose wire. She cried
then, shuddering, waking the baby.

The tractors didn't go for much, the cows,
once found, sold better, the auction drew more
than two hundred. People circled the trap
room and said what a fine-looking bride she'd
made, and how the little girl looked just like
her grandpa. But when Ernie showed up months
later to say she'd left for Montana,
that shocked them. All he had was the baby
and this dirty picture of the Virgin.

XII

And the ranchhand's so-called daughter? She grew
no way you'd think, raggy like the blue sage
even cows skip, not a tire tread against
drawn clouds, no John Deere beloveds rusting
heavenward. And she didn't grow wings to
satisfy whatever roan episode
myths shut on. She hunted for her mother
in more fertile quarter acres, and less,

in corn rows and pine forests, in lakes called
Mirror or Half Dollar, then she romanced
a park ranger to let her rappel down
the brow of one of those presidents. You
didn't read about it? *Oh father,* she
yelled, hugging him, *I'm not afraid of falling.*

Root Canal as a Venetian Idyll

The exhausted dream I live in
       is scattered with teeth, the little
           tombstones of Freud that,
plowed under,
          grow up warriors.

         My son buries his
between pillow and case so no one
       can exchange them for
foundling dollars —
          he wants to string them together,
          the miser.

The rule is you lose a tooth for every child.
       The new baby grinds,
     gnashes, butts
at the inexplicable ache inside —
          the dog that won't shake off.

      Yet he gums prettily between howls.
So smile! repeats his jack o'lanterned brother,
            as I do, falsely,
               as Death does.

JEAN/JEANNE BARET

Baret carrying ... even on those laborious excursions, provisions,
arms, and bulky portfolios of specimens with a perseverance and a
strength which gained for him from the naturalist the nick-name of
his "beast of burden."
> — JOHN DUNMORE, FRENCH EXPLORERS IN THE PACIFIC

I sailed high seas and low —
so plate-flat and hot the fish that flew
dropped and beat the deck.
Then I sunned,
though circumspect,
one pale limb at a time.
No one noticed what linked them:
this middle with none of a man's business.
I used a horn to make the proper arch with my water.

Five months. Halfway around.
I'd be the first. As inflated in their genius
as in the contents of their pants, all under
Bougainville
did not guess
save the plant man who gave me
salves to poultice a pregnancy,
and the thickest books
to bear across coral under noon suns.

But when the boils on my hands
burst, one of the males (by the plumage of the island)
laid a flower on it
and sniffed my neck —
he knew.

Just the books
banked against me kept him
from entering me.

                        I made my voice go deeper,
            I danced on his feet, I ran.

                        Alone on a spit a mile further,
I couldn't know that later
these islands would roast and eat white women
                if there was a question of whose:
                        easier to divide.

Rabbit-still,
            I stared at the ship, lagoon bound, bobbing.

                That night the sailors peeled
a coconut crab and found it red with egg

                                and ate it.
                I watered the plants.

                        On rumor, Bougainville himself
sent a man.
                We are loathe to err, he said.
The crew, from bosun down, laughed

                                then feared,
            a woman on board, and all that.
            I got the brig.

        Then two of the natives ate our mirrors
and their deaths made my sex
of less interest.

In weeks, syphilis showed itself

especially among those who did it,
as is the custom, in the open, in dance or song,
        the maidens, they said, forcing them,
            showing their *Ta-hee-tees.*

They would call out for their salves — *Jean, Jeanne.*

                                    We sailed.

No more sun shone for me
        until the specimen they took wanted a white
            woman.
Then I saw the sun —
        and ate rats after, chewing the tails down,
        their *merci.*

                        Bougainville said I'd be famous,
first woman around the world, and he
the first Frenchman. He made it sound like marriage,
                not history.
Then he threw out the anchor.
Here's an island, he said, *for you and the botanist.*

                        But I made it back.
                        The footnotes read:
She sailed for Madagascar
and married a planter.

            Planter? A few years on Marseille's dock
        strutting, rouged, with my mother,
and the future lifted — forget history.
It's all plunder for me and my pirate
partner.
                        There'll be a beard soon enough.

KARON

I am the girl
whom you thought
would be male and muscled
from shoving off, encountering
cataracts, sudden shoals,
all the other watercraft.
Forget it. We float
and I kick those who moan,
those who lean so far
toward the fading shore
I have to pull ballast
and protect the lines.
We do a lot of fishing
on the crossing — after all,
dreams are just carp
under the surface
and you've got to eat —
and eventually
there's singing to lead,
the handing out of oars,
and for some, the seasick pills,
all of which take time,
what I'm here to spend,
that last trickle down the tub
that goes so fast.
A girl is good for this,
a man, trouble. He thinks what
he sees will save him.
It's still like that.
When the white light business
breaks, all I say is
we've been through a fog.
I thrust in my pole, I pull.

BOTH IN AND OUT OF THE GAME
AND WATCHING AND WONDERING AT IT

for Scott Giantvalley

Over the convalescents' patio
                something peels,
either eucalyptus or smog-seared palm,
                and you brush it
from your bed jacket with a flourish
        from your schoolboy days,
                when to train a daddylonglegs
        up a girl's dress
wasn't for secondhand titillation
                        or torture
                but to vamp the *eek!*

Looking up into the usual blue,
        the everyday, nothing's-wrong blue,
                you recall another outdoors,
        your wedding, mother weeping —
                you saw that tear —
                        when you pricked your finger and put it over his
        to seal it,
                the only boy-on-boy ceremony.
The same old blood! The same red-running blood!

                It's okay, Dad, you wrote last week,
        forget that wages-of-sin chagrin,
no point punching out that kind of friend.
                        In L.A., you tell him, sometimes
                                ferns spring up
out of the mulching fossils
                        in the middle of the sidewalk,
                aberrant, luxuriant, still landscape.

        You decide to die in one of those decorator malls,
the Mercedes circling, honking, trumpeting

to get at your parking,
                    or at the beach,
blistering on one side, fish-white the other, steps
          from the musclemen and your mate
who allows you
                    the dignity.

                    You steady the leaves. The sun —
          there it goes —
promises nothing.
                    Day is done,
                    as in Scouts, that travesty,
and into his beard you go,
                    divine inside and out,
          still shameless,
and as weak
          as the laving ocean.

Skinny Dip

Eddies pull at my breasts.
From midstream, you are another

blossom, swaddled in that color
of cloth and sleeping, I hope,

on the bed of leaves I made for you.
Is the sand beneath you wet? I dive

to a warm spot, fish-breath-hot.
Almost too deep. I fear

not touching. My milk trails up
like octopus ink as a boat buzzes by.

Don't wake while I'm under.
My fingers, a mile off, beckon

but the broad palm anchors me.
When I hit the air

my skull's bones refit. Fish hatch
and swim away, so as I search the shore

I expect to see you rise from your blanket
and skim over the water,

and trout to snap in gladness.

TSVETAYEVA

Sent her two daughters to the orphanage
so they wouldn't starve. It took two weeks.

She was doing what was best. For whom?
She herself would die without love.

Who could hold a child that light?
The other couldn't talk.

She axed her wedding chairs
to bits so she wouldn't freeze,

then wept, grief good for what?
The bones and hair she came

to claim chained a noose
which worked wider and wider

until where she stood
didn't matter. Simple hunger.

DEATH STAYED

It feels like creation,
walking in on dogs
in their caged life and

pointing, that spark
ordained, God and man
joined as animals,

when we pick. Clouds
roll up and down the lot,
enchantment really,

as the dog jumps at my wrist
to kiss or tear. You open up
and tell me what it feels,

the third that makes the drama,
the queer addition
animals offer, our motion

of picking life off a seesaw
up now above the clouds,
the car climbing home,

our corporal selves
writ again,
with death stayed in a dog.

MIRACLES

A miracle in fact means work.
— WELDON KEES

                    Three ladies
                              run their Toyota
                    into the intersection against
the light.
                    One gray head-stalk sways out
                    as if checking the tires
                                        and shatters the window

                    as the young man's sports car
skids into them.

                    Standing in the glass she pats her hair
                                        and refuses
an ambulance. She wants *To get that boy.*

                    Exhaust smokes around her.

When something sweetens that part
which we grasp toward,
that patch of light that outlines
the masks on the wall
for no good reason,
the cavern bursting
out of
the cave's beleaguering twists,
concealment's required:
                    The Millionaire in silhouette,
                    never bemused or pitying,
his couriers as surreptitious
as melting ice.

           Yet the message must be as obvious
as a grocery label
because there are those signals we miss —
                    day and night,
                    meteorites fall all around us.
And if hypochondria is a wished-for disease
                    and the accident-prone are disturbed,
there are some who tend to miracle.

In a San Diego tract town
when crosses appear
on the bathroom walls —
I paid no attention,
before the reporters —
the miracle's like beauty
apprehended through a picture window,
attributed to pollution
and the house being set so
on the plot.

At most we're witnesses:
in Giotto's *Annunciation*
we're the disembodied hands
that arrow down to the groveling husband,
God about to cuckold him,
                    the saint/wife bent in prayer,
                         ecstatic against
the electric blue background,
                    just enough wind
                         against her garments
to suggest mistral,
                              what drove Van Gogh to his ear,
a Mediterranean persistence
that seeds the most barren
                    and topples the fertile.

But we can't hear the message,
the what for, the whisper.
Sex, you'd think, would tune us in.
                    Life we can pull out of test tubes
but you touch me there
and we're talking transport,
a tapping
                        of something bigger,
like Ben Franklin, his kite,
                his key,
the swami beckoning
the devotee,
                needing her
to complete the arc.

                        That first kiss recalls
that first kiss, mother's,
father's, Hans
with the milk-lined forelip,
                so stupidly romantic,
yes, highly colored by cinema-love
or bookish adultery
                        (the notepaper floating from the carriage)
yet evolving straight from
                        some proto-moment
essential to the species, beyond the yawn
                of Olduvai.

If that's not miraculous enough,
there's inspiration:
                the genius of glass
set in the holes of our houses,
                        the grooved disc full of music,
                        the iamb
                                that's been relegated

                    to the unconscious,
                            the winged chariot bumping
forward
in half-sleep,
                    the famous circle
of snakes forming benzene by themselves,
                    visions
just certain motes against certain light,
            inspiration more breath
than what keeps us
                            from whirling apart.
                    It's a comfort, not to believe more.

Why should we go down
on our knees
when it's our knees
we want to worship?

We stand at the mountaintop
and shout
who, who, who
for the echo —
                    the truth of Narcissus
that we are not water,
                    the lie of the tombstone
that it returns us,
                    molecule by molecule —

compels us to circle
            the bulbed models,
the mated salts.
        We have science clutched to our breast
like a lily,
                    we are the Pharaoh
            laid in the most propitious

                    shaft of starlight.

        We believe the waterfall's
stopped
                    because a little girl
sits on the stream
or that Guadeloupe's church
                        protrudes from the lava
because that's what's tallest.
                                Science:
what we see is all there is.

But then it happens:
What do you want?
the doctors shout without opening their mouths,
                    a miracle?
                        We're dumb too,
for the child
is dying,
is dead,
                    a small, slight body
trapped in the lower left hand corner
of this bare green room
while the EEG tickertapes triumphant
arrival elsewhere,
                        binds
what's left behind.

Three days pass.
We start to think
the Pied Piper can't get them all,
                    his tune falters — surely we were
        thankful enough, a child's
that kind of miracle.

But the stone is all we have of sanity.
                    We don't want it pushed back,
the corpse coming unwrapped,
dream-naked, terrified.

No. The miracle must be a little bell
in the back garden, coming out of silence,
not the gong
that sets us tumbling.

HEALING WIND

That's upwind, where
genealogy has swept its O's
and X's beyond

hugs and kisses.

This week is not
the last, your sister implores.
We stand at the tap, pails

filled, the wind in ruffs
so no reflection
shows. She's not especially

cold but the chill index says it all:
worse than you think.

No one cries.

Why
tempt sisterliness
when there's loss to carry back, lots
of it.

We heft and tuck our heads.

Captain Andy

Leave me be. From here on the veranda
I watch a path that's not slimed by slugs
nor soiled by rabbits, the damn brown rabbits
pausing in their gnawing, nor the high stink
of daisies, but one that's combed sand, palm, crab.

What light there is mottles my hands into
sealskin, dumb critters I killed for a time,
so merrily. With just a tap, their chops
turned quite violet, a singer's color.
Not me, nor my wife, Ngarima, could sing,

though her love tunes — whew! Crescendo,
real crescendo. To me she's *Anemone*
for how her legs flail. Why do words
at the end get better? Shouldn't they get stuck
up in the pump as it rusts? In this light

I'm on my boat, a swan's back.
That's the English in me, the swan. Better
a re-fined shark. Like all sailors, I hate
the water and anything in it.
First time I clippered was after flogging

Victoria's death. Oh, a boat in black,
crack-silent, the sailors doffed — there's the soul.
Then I weathered a grand typhoon. Too young
for women (begging your pardon), I drank
double rum as we wallowed down. Since that

wasn't the end, I changed. After suchlike
some men float in their eye juice, tide to tide.
Only a stirring in the groin tricked me
into coming about, my Ngarima.
She's a strong wind, she filled me. We traded

a schoonerful of string, hooks, lemon drops.
Might as well as been the goddamn family ferry
since we stuck to ports with sisters
and grass huts. I went fat as a porpoise
on good bream. But this is no life story:

there's a point, that these Polynesians
sail to the pull of their balls, not string maps.
That's all cat's cradle. And their balls are wrong.
How often I've hauled them in! They laughed when
I stuck my hand into the sky as if to

hold on. The right stars always steered my dreams,
so the booming at midnight was the reef
and not the bottom of the boat, a sound
as sickening as a child's night cough.
Stars bored into me as I humped on deck

with all the lamps off or got tied to the mast,
for penance. That's why the bed's out here.
I got to see my way. Change sixty years
of star-towing just for a little dying?
Put out the light. I can smell their burning.

New: All the Livelong Day

ONE

ALL THE LIVELONG DAY

                             The train loses track.
Crime, your sweetheart, makes me
look good anyway. I'm outstretched,

        the girl given. Who tied my bonds?
This is a New Year,
people swig
                on the sidelines, people
                turn away.
                        Gawd, I say.

There's a couple more like us,
           they come out of my body while
                I wait, *choo-choo*,
                            time
hugging the course, the bend gravy,
the bed heroic, someone sawing
                      at the bonds,
           cinders swirling at
           a cow caught on the catcher,
           bearing down.

O fingers, faster.
                  No one will remember
          my name or yours, only
                         the humming, the talk-
      into-the-distance song, and Crime's,
           ticketless
all the livelong day.

Heart-Shaped Candle Scenario

Darling, he says. *I love your little wick.* He sidles up to her opaque self, his heartbeat fast. If lit, her heat would be just enough to snap his FBI airlock tight and sigh and smoke. But exciting titles scroll over her while she casts her meaningful glance: beware the louvered doors. He looks and looks and finds – a bunch of birds between his loins. Explosion. Then he's running, electrons flashing, a knife between his teeth. Cut to at-home Italians. Make that Sicilians, make that with killer anchovies. Nobody speaks da English, nobody's gonna turn her in. They don't care if he is da Pope. Does he want an extra slice with that knife? He flees to his console for consolation, he iPuds and Wiis up the wazoo, he Sims and Half-lifes, he can't get anything going in the fancy computer effects department. Then the heart-shaped candle saunters her waxed self past and it's the chaste scene: she twitches her mouth, so European. *Fetch this,* she says and *I'll melt.* Soon he hangs from a clockhand — but the clock is digital. *Bitch,* he whimpers. Meanwhile she finds dry sticks and rubs them slowly, oh so slowly, and thrillions of pixels burn, burn with misunderstanding, the crowds between them in their clean costumes soon dirty from more explosions and car crashes. Lots of blue light where he lands in an empty warehouse full of smoke, where he hammers and hammers to find a way out. So many other heart-shaped candles — Italian? Sicilian? — rush in under the exit sign he can't find, so many he can't read their meaningful lips. Whose arms to run into, which one has the gun? Helicopters, AK-47s, a broken bridge dangling over a roaring cataract, an airplane embarrassed by winglessness. Then he spots her, puddled in the driveway — violins — and presses his face into her warm wax to FBI her into heart-shape at last.

REPORT FROM THE PRAIRIE

Lots and lots — think square feet, Tess D'Urbervilles
(skip the *of the* — too local) says on her cell,
and the place is really pretty treeless. Maybe prairie,
she posits. What it needs is a cow.
She should've run the other way, Greece
or Macedonia at least but

hey, she didn't end up sharing a cell
or having people get all prayer-y
over her mother who is having a cow
because she's not married. Plenty of grease
needed for that wheel. A big butte
affixes the scenery, Indians' or vil-

lains' arrows pricking the pseudo-prairie.
Lord, she complains, *cow-*
ards everywhere. Two weather geeks
give her her next ride. Miss Tess
is not long in spotting a discarded drug vial,
but neither carry on like Vin Diesel.

Instead, new arrows kill a cow
she hadn't noticed that the two greas-
y guys from maybe Nebraska-abut-
ting Edinburgh fight over, the Deauville
tornado-chased so far in hopes of a cable sell
now pooped out in the midst of whatever prairie.

Prancing around them like a Greek
goddess, she asks if at least they have smokes but
the short one, unfamiliar with vill-
anthropy, refuses. The tall one's glands, on a cell-
ular level, beam red. *That's eerie,*
she mutters, and takes an arrow. *The cow's*

bleeding, he shrieks. The short one laughs but
says quick, *No offense. Vile*
nudniks, she shrieks, frightening the prairie
dogs into cats. *Where's Stonehenge?* Cow-
ed, the two point. *Grok*
where Homer hammers albacore cell-

by-cell-tender with rocks? one bleats. *But*
he's not my type, she wails.
Hardy knows I never do Greeks.

DOVE-WHIRR

Dove-whirr in the theater of morning
                                    not mourning, not yet,
        though the single locust shakes out to be
a snake
        and the car lengthens into
a limo the wrong color.

                    Anyway,
what about
                        the dog?
        O Peaceable Kingdom,
as quaint as you are,
                    such days
we have had, the corn we are now, rowed,
        with a perspective
                    that vanishes. Our shoes are tied.

        But smoke reaches.
                    I'm no one, we say, over and over,
with our oxygen. We slink, cocktail dress by
                dress, into girl positions,
wearing black already.
        Goof up now and the dryer
                    will tumble on in darkness.

ANTIGONE WINS

Out of the house, insists the doorbell —
Antigone's confessed. O, what to wear
for the coffin. O, Greek hair.

Nobody answer, Dad says, *nobody
get the door.* Indisposed and evil,
he lets the sentry stew.

What ho from the back window?
Is sister tattling on sister?
Is it her *Me too*? Speak up,

get the sword out of mothballs,
break the anvil's cartoon fall.
We're a family, sister says at last,

for godsake, get the door.
Is it a sparrow beaking crumbs
stuck beneath the bell,

a god's loud *Yes*,
the Greeks sobbing
at every rent black shroud,

or the boyfriend, searching for the end?
Go ahead, forbid mourning.
There's always *déshabillé.*

Rock 'n Roll

A weak bird sings *Dusk* while the email scripts *Wait!*

A girl rolls over in her skates, falling beachwise.
You know

she bleeds, *ahhhhh*, unlike
the bird,
a stepped-on toy we bought at Goodwill.

It's another front page
that pronounces her bikini *slaver on toast.*

                                        Waiting to read it
is the new smoking. *Send?* A Danish
with loquat is one in the bush. He waits.

She adjust the signature line,
heels over head. Who will fly?

The script
wishes to restate: *My goodness, my morals.*

        There in the dusk, a goodwill wheel.
Pronounce walk, not roll. Better, text it.

P-E-N-I-S,

Acrostic means tip of the verse *in Greek.*

I.

P is for prehensile and projectile. Anatomy stretching — wrenched — toward, in petition.

E is for enervated, the skin thwarted, hidebound, so expressive.

N is for notices every naughty every 7 minutes. In pre-efflorescence, commands native tongues.

I is too much with us, that exclamation, *if this then* a whole army of I, interested and alert, i-penised, informational, each iconic.

S is for sperm, seraphim shouting *Salubrious!* in salute.

II.

We're staring at an illustration at the sex museum. Shocked.

Y chromosomes, carried only by male humans, have been losing genes and shrinking. A small elite force remains resilient. Even when a species loses its Y chromosome, there are cases in which it will avoid extinction by acquiring a new system to determine gender, like the Ryukyu spiny rats.

Penis 1: With powerful, easy to use tools.
Penis 2: Lock and key?

You wouldn't believe Jimmie is different ... till he showed you ... you wonder if God has spoiled him. — Lola Ridge

Why not the arms or the adenoids?

HAIRY STREAMS

You could hike over them, the you
without a problem, the heights
viewed from the convenient closet
coats are shed in, your constant
Yes/No a hee-haw, a mule alert
that's pasture-perfect,

a coronary at the last corner.
Nobody's framing the chintz-
covered wall to cover the leak.
Besides, you like leaks, you're inside
the view as if hibernating
or crazy, you try not to erupt.

Hypothesize the rest,
the languor and freshet,
the crags, the serrated parade.

So — mountains? What about hairy streams,
the pushed-up bushes saying, *Pet me?*
You got a problem? No.
Cascade is what we call it,
a voice off the hanger, the blouse
cast in a corner or animate.

APASSIONATA

The Murphy bed talks, falling
out of the wall. *Wait a snake,*
it says. *Don't forget where*
the ovaries stand. A brass band
wakes us early if we haven't
been had. There's a pill to swallow,
not the bitter one. Strung in a line —
pill, pill, pill — you're sated and counting.
You bought them online.

Tra-la, the proto-children take apart
their limbs, a whole chicken
spit and roasted. You drive around
for the pieces, risking heat.
Ah, children, the physiological
point of passion unless
it's chasing butterflies. If not
Freud-bound, muscled.
Cheat the heat, don't ovulate.

The Extremes sing: *no kids here.*
Hefner-heavy, slick magazines
chart their terrors. Don't sniff
the seam. Everywhere there's
dalliance, brilliance and chance.
You could take it standing or
mounted right now, with wings
on lift, with its impossible
formula you forget after the test.

Girls on one side, boys anywhere.
The mountain flaps its *Come here*
to both, and *Concentrate.* The game
is turning over pairs, is remembering
to turn. A Big White Lie whirls in,

a wall but see-through. Trouble is
anywhere there's want and need
that's separate. Please be, the peepers
cheep, I've got rhythm.

You've got what it takes because
passion holds its breath, a big one.
Scandal wears itself out, pointing.
That finger gets genderized —
what a blender! The ice cracks
into smoothies, cold smiles: *See this*
on every tongue, hoping no one
does, and everyone. You've got
breath to take away, spleen.

FUSION CONSTRUCTION

The sun shows it off.

What you actually see is electrons on a newsreel,
the extra-hot Soviet Tokamat
in the shape
        of a torus — you know — donut.

"Most magnetic bottles are inherently unstable — says Teller
(not Penn &)
            at the Princeton Gun Club. (Skeet, anyone?)

Lasers, those guns, curse the darkness.
        Or denseness.
Call it Shiva,
                BIG SCIENCE.

ZETA claims this, ZETA claims that.
Cold fusion announced but why?
                    No one can prove it.
Ditto acoustic cavitation
on a tabletop   though it sounds like Astaire.

        They build a basket but
fuel must eat something:
time, this time.

        Big logs
get lifted, an animatronics
of change, a mechanical water buffalo (up come skyscrapers)

— nice Handel, hear it under
the voiceover? — but Babel bubbles up:
EURATOM, START, MAST, JET, NIF, ITER, FIRE, EAST,
SPRFD, (Fire Department?), a Z machine,
the current world record of Q,

plus irrational fear, unwarranted
code, another country's   penis.
Change requires copulation,
nakedness, pleasure   the sunny egg
under bombardment.

Eat
the coxcomb and the sun will not rise.

Two

SANDWICH

Across the stage of the plains interstate inter state dell and dell and plains, there is a scene where they run out of gas.

You — in the white shirt —

I'm just as scenic. Listen: *There was a tremendous knocking.*

Knock, knock.

No joke. They put him in a closet.

Not a dell?

They put him in a closet and the door, hung wrong, had a gap at the bottom where you could shove a whole sandwich through, though the bread got a little dirty. As for thirst, I don't know. No light of course except through the gap so the sandwich came in dark and dirty.

Whispering voices from the phone.

Can you get it?

There was a tremendous knocking across the plains, sometimes as if on a windowpane. Sometimes enough to break it, or else from below.

You don't know that.

It's a kind of knowing, just like the knocking you say you heard just after they ran out of gas. And who is the they anyway? The usual suspects, M and F, old while you're not and because of that, always running out of gas.

They wished there were windows. There were sandwiches they made for themselves, they didn't shove them all.

The door will be open. But that means mud will be tracked in by the gas-less, earning alienation.

Time gaps while they run away like that, after someone finds him in the closet. Maybe the someone went looking for a coat, a winter coat that he thought he had hung in there. Pee-You.

M and F forgot their homemade sandwiches and they ran out of gas.

How do you know?

Someone called. Someone said, *Look in the closet.*

It was you.

I was wearing a white shirt, easy to spot. I didn't need a coat.

They walked a long way before anyone picked them up, and it never stopped raining. The dell came up while they were walking. A farmer in the dell. A big Ford truck with 4WD.

Interstate.

No trace of footsteps because of the rain.

Interstate gets into the car like a hum. You would think they were fleeing the site but no, they just ran out of gas.

What if guilt is free like the falling of rain instead of cooped up in a closet? He was crying.

I'm not related. I'm not the last or the late. I'm not — really.
I say: there was a scene and someone went inside but whether —

A white shirt is easy enough to spot. Dirt just falls on it.

There was a tremendous knocking.

The Wait

The cloud versus home / colonial dream of mobility versus decolonial construction

safety in numbers / gendering of public spaces

itinerant scholar / the safe itinerant / the itinerant artist

the insecurity of mobility / gender / sexuality / race in transit and across borders

from passport checks to biometric mobility controls

ticketing systems / E-Ticketing / E-Terror

the price of speed / the cost of easy border crossing

mobile public space / from public to corporate transit / public interstitial space

the promise of mobility / disability and access / access

LIFESPAN

Fake the dark storm over the light,
                      fluff cast as drama, two men
           in track suits instead of
hefting poison spears.
            Admit choice, not fate,
           the crashplan hoisted
out of the trashpit where no
                   peanuts spew
           from the bag. Order the ordure
      if you have to.

Also eschew January that forces
             you to ennoble your feet, watch every step,
        not skip. The poet shakes her finger
           but it already shakes for a coda,
for a *What's this?* Let it snow
        as if it's a gift you didn't order, you can't send back, you've lost
           the receipt, you saw more at that woman's postmodern
                  reception.
Terrible reception.

SO NOT DEAD

(Nevermind, nevermind. *The Ballad of Lazy Jane?*)
(No. Two porkchops almost raw? Yes.)

(If waves meet out there, do fish turn around?)
(That's the kind of question you don't answer *booze.*)

(*Au revoir*, in a language I smear.)
(If the waves meet. How dumb. Not
even Zen.) (As if I knew a lick about Zen —

it's a coin I'm spending.)
(A ballad is deceptively easy to write.)
(As in deceit.)
(As in undeserved.)
(Cynicism reduces the charge of sadness.)

(Jane had heart disease, lupus, she was slow.)
(The fish drank too much.)
(France perfected goodbye.)
(Zen is all about waiting)   (Pathetic.)

(Parenthetically, my father is standing by)

(that is, dying, after years and years)
(A ballad about a woman who lived on the smell of roses.)
(A ballad about very fat men.)

(There's doom in everybody. That's what the waves
go on about.)   (Doom, doom, doom.)

                    (Don't be silly, Jane's windows are closed
     so she can't —)

                    (I didn't tell her to —)

                    (She didn't —)

                              (No more pink chops.)

(Dad's still alive, but very fat.)

                    (Not me, say the waves, meeting

                    in mid-ocean, fish missing.)

     (*Au revoir.*)

                              (A *revoir* you can't miss.)

MORE FOOD

Light clots then slides into the dark parking lot, making a number
of stops along the way, how we progress as inhumanly and
unadvisedly as anyone we might be sorry to see, even the son.

What's that about the sun we meant to raise? Or the way out being
the in? The inn is closed, the lovely inn, the foreign house with its
distant Japanese cuteness and the volcano as cute as it is

toppling its red over the sun on the flag, as in the son about to
venture forth, wrath and might, a lot of that, and the Mac truck
bearing down a bad grade in front of him, no salt to make

the grip good. A bad grade, every word wrong, then pop, the happy
light of day under an umbrella nobody said would hold off water,
the water holding, the driver laughing at the turn,

me beating the son with the spokes for what? You'll never know, the
oak with its nuts hitting the squirrels until they beg for mercy, not
more food, the oak not so far from the big acorn.

There's a Closet for That

I've got the locks off, nothing but screws in my pocket. And three magnets. *Don't smile,* I say into my hand — *those are stuck screws, they aren't loose.*

He's cute, says Fran. *I could eat two of him.* I'm at the bassinet but she's watching *Animal Planet,* the channel of ambitious dogs and smart pigs. *Why would a baby not ever cry? What was wrong with him?*

I said that.

There's a bean in a Dixie cup I want to go back to, my kid drowned it because I said *Good, good.* Sometimes opinion is better, discourse.

I've known Fran for what she would say eons. I had to call and call this time to get her over. *There's a marathon outside, on TV,* she says. *It makes me feel lazy.*

Tuna for three. My kid tells me about mercury, he's written a paper on it, he's unstocked our cupboard and measured his intake. *Too much* is about right. *Where did I get it?* Fran isn't eating anything with eyes — she's that kind of friend.

No one should have to bear ketchup on the face for too long. I mean the watcher, the other diner with his own ketchup problems. I reach over an invisible wall and swipe the visual to *Good.* The tuna the dog's eating.

He goes off to catch a plane after lunch and I have to find a box, tape, postage. It's his best whatever he's left behind. I send it not because I'm Mother-for-a-Day but because he could get sad, too sad.

When I say sad I mean terminal. One false move or even one move that could be false on top of another half false, and maybe not enough water.

Fran likes her drugs color-coordinated. *Reminds me of the Impressionists,* she says. *Seurat. Vitamins you can count on.* She is discreet with her gold-and-seashell tiny box. Nitroglycerin is what they took in the twenties.

My kid calls Fran *Also Ran.* It's not like he has a sense of humor, he's accurate. But he has his own history. All you have to do is roll up that shirt he left behind on that arm of his.

Made you look, he'd say.

If I'm watching my screen, I don't see the bassinet taking up half the room because even eBay won't buy it but what I do see is upsetting: I've inputted my social security number instead of my password. I'm old enough. Fran doesn't laugh either. I say, *Let's fix something.*

The screws get gunned into the closet. My neighbors beat on the door and take that gun away. *What?* They can't hear the marathon casualties on the TV.

We eat burgers at a place a block from home, ketchup staining the paper napkins. My kid's back, the terminal's terminal, no planes out. He walked all the way back *because it was fun,* he says, with his no-cab sarcasm, who says I don't know shit about bombs.

A closet full of shirts, of the arms separate and flying. Fran can't go anywhere either. Outside there's the high beams of cars, traffic we never have, sirens and real suffering.

Say, I say, when we get home, *I still have the magnets.* He snaps his screen shut.

THE PORTRAIT

Not flattering, executed less with love than frustration:

Hold still!

      Pigtails, dazed eyes and
         paint: orange, green, brown.

         I take the painting off
the wall, bequeathed. No — she said nothing about it but
         nothing too
about giving it
to the others.
            I should be happy:
      I got to watch TV.

         Gretel's behind the door,
             the others
are lined up like trussed chickens
         or snow fellas, sorrow
         cold and clumped,
            waiting to melt
inside.

        Answer the door, they can hear the TV's on,
answer the door, they want
to pose too.

         The paintress arrives
turpentine-fingered.
      Could burst into flame.
      Could, this time, in the time she has,
         paint.

Don't look at her, I warn them,
look at your future: the TV.

      Lined up outside the door, they say

they've drunk the turpentine, she could paint
with their very bodies.
The oven is so hot
they might explode.

On the other hand, I could be an artist, I like the smell.

She stares at the canvas:
My nose is not right.

Let me be someone,
I say to the brush, *Let me be,*
through this,
someone.
I move.
She curses.

Paint streams off the canvas onto the heads
of the others who are still
crying.
Tell them I'm painting,
she says. I shout:
she's painting,
moving only my lips.

The TV blanks with its *Star Spangled Banner* she paints so long.

I look right enough to me.
Right? she laughs.
It's how you look, she says.

The others tongue the frost on the windows,
bang with the kindling.
Look at me, they say,
each with his own face pressed close.

It's mine she paints over and over.

                    The others now with
children of their own, with their own faces.

                    The portrait still
of a girl who never saw
                    who painted her,
just the light from the screen.

SWAN PLAY

You were the swan-necked one who rode.
—THOMAS HARDY

Bells from a church, and a friendly dog.
She she she like a goddamn sweeper.
The lamp is on, it's that dark. Clothes on a sofa,
chips he could stick his hands into.
Her shoes are off. What's at stake?
The door is the best he can do.
At last the bleat — car — bleat.

The sting of that goodbye, the lamp off,
the chips crushed, the sofa empty.
She keeps finding that door. It's getting late.
Where are the keys? The bird at its bars.
Who's there? she bleats, sweeping
the bell to the floor. His hand catches hers,
but not under his clothes.

Half a life gone, the door ajar, her clothes
off, entered every which way, the bird
swanning the mirror he can almost
see from the couch. The dog barks
its likes, there's a bag of chips but
that want has to wait. The keys ring,
hitting the floor. The car, too early.

The door's stuck. He's eating the bird,
the chips left for the sweeper. Her face darkens.
The dog asks for a stick. She's got it.
Whose couch is it? The keys, the bills,
the clothes, the car — take them.
The crushing beat: *Good.* The heart,
discarded, staining the sofa.

The bag prissy, its combed clasp unripped,
every chip crisp, the vacuum behind the door.
She shoehorns his heart, sets it on the couch,
clicks the lamp but it doesn't go on.
It's not that late. The key's in the laundry.
Damn! She shakes it loose. The doorbell rings.
The swan, just in time, mute.

NO EMERGENCY

The sirens scream past my ear:
           thirty-two years and he reveals —

                    the sirens inhale, drop the ash
of cigarettes in a hiss.
He says

a cruise on a shoot is a temptation
in a marriage that was over
before the line left the dock. (previous
marriage).

                    The cameras he directed
were set: the why of desire
growing green
against the blue horizon, the pool and its waves —

a little land. She sang.
                    Decades swim by,
three of need and whisper,
sidelong glances that suggest
the past
comes as unbidden as desire,

                    the smoke of a secret so old
it's almost

uxorious.
Say the movie was never released,
the critics went elsewhere, the woman
                              (women)
left behind in an embrace I know better,
I now know less.

CURRENT AMBITIONS

In America (as if the Empire —no,
too obviously left — as in the City —)

MONSANTO GROWS FLOWERPOTS
citizens
(illegals [in corporate talk] with their rights,
net octopi like Greeks (money
grows in banks on rocks) (or Homer giving us

the Iliad, giving us the odd Odyssey))
that is,
creatures more legged than ourselves
(most cephalopods frozen, from Asia)

ANGELINA BEARS TWIN BEARS
aliens
from the deep
(shallows, octopi swim
right over to the hankie he flutters)
submerged,
and used for bait, not
(the Japanese word for obnoxious)
breakfast, yet
in America
some dew-slick (what color?) freak
from NASA
[see THE PLANS] scrabbles o'er the moon or
an elsewhere
MAN FALLS ON ORB
so unmarked and unmanned
the crabbed prints hither/
thither

invokes animal   terror
(See rabbits.)
GUN TAKES GLUM

Grok? [What about] America
in motion, its bursts —

          BREADLINE HEADLINE
          (Somalia, Somalia) some
or all its *Yeah Yeah* accumulating,
relating   iterative

     LAST STRAW FOR EUROPE
thrusts (see Mama) NASA-
esque, the big envelope

out there
        SALE! SALE! SALE!
boneless intelligence
           (the U.N. rallies). We text

America, Amerika, Amerigo (the franchise)
        but the captcha can't be,
          letters
all octopi and dark and wet   even
Biblical
      THE END HAS NEARED
          yet key
to contact. Line-up and vacuum,
              line-up —
take names
        the U.N. has its rally *(Babel!)*
        unscrew childproof caps

and the desert, Forty Days in [name of good franchise]
        looms. Las Vegas?
               Dissent and fasting.

WHEEL CABBIE AWAY
Google translate.

198

MONEY STANDING AROUND

Capillaries and leucocytes tingle
as the great banks of blood
busy themselves, sloughing
and harrowing our insides.
I'm not writing *like money.*

Statistics show the great fiscal decisions
are most often made by whim,
not women. The world nods.
The great bear and bull act,
animal rights aside,

insists on the curtain: *We agree*
honey/money/funny.
I'm not explaining all I know.
Wads kept in the freezer
groan for acronym,

CD/IRA/SEP/KEOGH,
instruments that play well
at a certain tempo, as long as
no fireman checks for ice cream,
the smoking cables

ATMing through the walls,
hoses all the time about power.
I'm not holding my breath,
I'm not even shaking my head
if barter's revived.

Consider the Predator droning
overhead, surgically, as it were,
striking — there's money falling.
You hide your house number,
your ZIP code, your expiration date.

Money ebbs in a meadow:
the bear unshot for dinner,
the witnessing trees exchanging air,
the air not acid out of agreement.
Evil so often remains: the box unchecked

but the cookie set, the crowds
cajoling the man to jump,
an abstract hand at his back,
or the chief ordering his men to shoot,
then everyone wet from what's shed.

HOW TO MAKE MONEY FIERCE

Granted, we're cycling
across the earth, then recycling,
the wheel soon enough dropping off
as coin, the Roman head twirling
to a stop, someone's hand slapping it down —
less energy than gravity.

Four lambs slain for two sheep,
a bargain to please both parties,
more meat. Death's not always involved,
the worn shroud exchanged for a plaid,
sometime it's *Smile* and there's two more plums.
But the plums get eaten, the girl given,
the relatives offer bad milkers.

How to make money fierce, the love of your life?
He's in a trench coat, the belt tight,
his briefcase bulges, he speaks
with egregious sadness: *Our fathers
who art in heaven, thank god.*
The cinchy comments after, all about desire —
I don't want to describe it.

FUEL ADIEU!

Once, living as a seal,
I leapt the margins of waves
into sunsets made green by lichen.

You buy that? The tiny plants,
the angle of the sun, the seal?
Atlantic City tidies itself

into the margins of waves
nobody watches or they'd
miss their dice roll. If you

lichen on Facebook the box
unlichens, living living living
on margins really singular

for the green electricity
that meets its demand, the seal
no-friended on account of

gamboling on lichen — it could be
algae without the fuel —
and myself an impersonator,

a drop of oil in the shape
of the surface gasping
for what I can get,

a sunset, a wave, a lorgnette
to see the cards being dealt.
I can swim into the sunset

anthropomorphized or not,
the margins set regardless
of perspective, the seal

sunk, the lichen changed
into phosphorescence
as if a wave goodbye.

Adieu! the seal says with its tail,
an extension of its waist. The waves
okay that, the sun *likes*.

MERENGUE

Hey feet, it's a sweaty world. Night lives between

    beats, cat-stretch, ready to wild. But

                      too
      articulate, like words
spilled
after *like*, matching phrases

    sense-chained and hollerable,
  toe-tap evil.

         The leg swans out,
    the scarecrow wades button-high
into a quick
twist.
        He's asleep, the girl guesses,
      shoulder kissing,

and the frame of the step
    shifts.
        A cut-away of the notes
      reveals the hammer to anvil:

music made, wrung and wrought,
          the poor thumb stung.

Left feet, right. How many does a bee
    wield, high on the rhythm of *Go?*
             Pollen

      heavy, the singer sneezes and the song's
off.

Where were you going anyway? Heaven

           is furious, its envy

angels
fall into.

DYSTHYMIA

Out of the bright day, a dark.
No dodging swallow at dusk.

Wrist-ache, mouth dry, god knows —
dilated pupils. Who learns woe?

Leaden stairs flowing down,
hair awry, clothes all clown.

Every *Yes* tinged, every *Why* suspect.
The trees bend away, sighs check

or elongate. Spit won't season it.
There's no reason for it, there's no credit.

THREE

Please Please Me

Hothouse ritual: live coding, tele-robotics, net-art. Release early and
often

and with many a
> home-made dream machine, encoded charm &
> fem-botics. This is notorious R&D.

Study power structures by tracing the flow of packets as they pass
over land and sea.

> Make macro-economic and geo-strategic speculation.

But

when we spend most of our lives online,
> connected, who are the *we?*

Mass online swarms begin and dissipate.

Beyond the screen
alliances obscure the between-you-and-machine.
Among.

Harp and the Machine

Insert travel narrative here,
humans as machines refuting laws
like Einstein's, traveling dimensionally in threes,
chord, triage, ménage a trois,
the Holy Family waving their flat little lives:
Pick me! Pick me! There's a harp

machined to play *Dead*
is all you get. Lift those legs,
dry that lichen, to whatever tiniest
congregation ends up stopping,
relatively speaking. This harp
is hunted and pecked. One string of gut

goes *pluck* then 3,000 Chinese workers
assemble under one roof, a bullet ballets
into a chamber, the chamber becomes a war.
I was there too. Here, the dialogue,
the interrogation. Press the tear duct,
apply pressure, witness away —

it's not enough. *We love everyone!*
With more prong effort:
the bent penis, the sleight of finger,
the hand over the eyes, the harp
vibrates further into the skull, it resorts
to distortion: a gravity-shaped arpeggio,

a terrible smile looped through time,
a kind of scallop or private part
repeated along the bedroom wall
asking, *Why the repeat?*
Because Einstein plucked it so.
Time and distance,

the heart growing less fond.
The boy runs so hard
that injury comes to him,
it swishes up like a trademark,
he falls and his own teeth
pierce his lip in neat scallops.

Allegro, the sprite who handles
the boy's weeping with a broom,
keeps a hallowed horse, its soft ears
twittering to the music outside.
Insert live animal here, on a gurney,
leg broken, muzzle screaming.

Part of me says, *Pardon me?*
What I hear are the ducts and the drums,
the cantilevered. Einstein rolls up
on Constellation-X, his pot belly pressing
relativity's, and GPS groans,
its satellites lag. Insert prong for cantilever.

But the whine, the *there* there,
the harp *andante* all the way down
to mere lichen, posits rock, a smash.

Riviera Terrors

Plug in a tree,
      palm even, the bird —
make it black, not
          raven but ravenous,
            loud in the palm
upside down as in an Escher
      of village life
         (a few people walk the hills,
under bridges)
         the plant perpendicular at least,
           a concession.

A blue car presses the nap
              of macadam
         fresh dripped.
You've pressed that button
         and the bird's wings sticky,
         why it's so hungry
         and loud.

The blue car
         out of a Hitchcock flick
    (scream that)
           where color
    is fierce (dream that)

    and the back halves
of olive groves menace.
            (see the game
your son plays)

         Audio: the laundry.
         Audio: chair scrape.

(don't forget the bird)

       Ocean + ocean + ocean
       both up and down, the way
              gravity can surprise you —
the horizon.
           The plate of it, as blue
       as the streaming car
               full of fish as devious
       as *Notorious,*
          (the plate, not the car)
upends.

       You have to amass land
       to perturb,
             the anger and ardor kept under
oil and water
       that the bird has its beak full of
               below, the fish eating each other —

       (Picture that:
       dogfish eating dogfish.)

K. KHAN

Some bent hook of a child
carries a lantern into his dream,

one foot gold, the other paste,
a derangement of touch.

He's slow, penis tucked,
broad shoulders humped,

the way forward a basalt cave.
A sound —

the dream lunges, the light goes
end over end, and he whimpers.

Oh, palimpset of fever and loss,
your ague never quenched,

quench, quench, quench,
the dream reaches down and eats

the forever child, a delicacy.
The dark calls out, *why?*

in a life of sleep. Wine-daunted,
the boy-turned-man wakens

with the name, cast out when
the lantern fell. He tells me.

WHAT DAY IS TODAY?

Not enough has been made of the barking dog at dawn.
Precipitate the agitate, says one to the other,

Let's talk alarmist, or *Bravo, the laurels are scattered* or

Re-signify the world, one lawn at a time. Don't let birds do it.
It is, after all, another blank day to scrawl with howls.

Be-thy-name! Then silence, a trap, all ears pricked.

Morning's Hie

Weak plants stalk themselves to the sun that's out out out,
the sun victimizing the eyes scanning

the deck for these weak plants or rest. The rest,
arrested in photosynthesizing positions,

planted with riot in their leaf tips and tabby contentment,
file away the heat. Hot to the feet.

I deck-watch for weather, uncertain that that color
really glows or if the flower's on fire

because the criminal in me who rises post-
sleep wants to know who did this and why can't I?

and will wreck the racheting bird-song
signaling the end-of-berries the plants barely hold up,

a heaviness that grows with a bird's investigation,
as stern as a window, as one that gets closed.

SEASONED

Only three wise men? Or — so many?
A dove flock never touches down
or touches each other.

Snow piles on its beards
Plenty of cars then, car-a-van,
peace symbols, the seats taken out.

Abruptly He rises, has His nails hammered,
swaddling dangling. His mother cries.
Kings, like Martin Luther, replace the hand-wringers.

But it's still just desert. *No corn,* cries the donkey.
None, let alone trees evergreen.
Yet *Hark!* the vowels sing, a karaoke of seraphim.

Their wings — two lungs — dim the day
with vanished breath. The cold sees its own.

ARCHILOCHUS

Among the cloud gods, the wind's applause,
curtain and orchestra, the Greeks'

in particular, its rulers as needy as
this goat giving the horizon kicks.

I'm a stick walking cross island
comparing myself to the clover, straining

its wildness into chlorophyll, myself suitably
green with retsina, though the drink's

hard to find, pitch isn't flowing
like the yogurt and honey. Suitably I'm one

foot at a time, teetery over rocks that slaves
settled into place, who walked back over these rocks

to their hovels under the same bright blue
with their *I*s, passing the ancient poet,

the first to posit a singer
his own song, to sing he's no hero.

LIBRARY RESCUE

A war or an attack — why don't I
go on the _____? Smoke everywhere, I
can't find my way, I
fall through a door, a library. I
squat hiding, hair so much longer. I
find a book, I
open it to the flap — my face. I
try to convince a man it's me, I
don't think he's you, I
let him take me home but I
am not his, I

look around at the cul de sacs and cubbies in this underground
what — a doctor's warren of waiting rooms, then a room full of
food. More blasts while I'm thinking I could find parking down
here, I could find my car. I don't panic. Maybe it's geological,
maybe it's mining but as smoke and alarms fill the air, people
disappear where before they sat in chairs with their mouths open. I
should have gone to where you and my son —

I run but I can't get out, men rush into corridors just the width of
their bodies. I hide in the threshold of door after door, but I can't.
When they find me, they have no expression, they have mine.

They try to take a book away from me and I won't give it. When the
small man, as threadbare as war, thrusts out his hands to take it by
force, I lean forward in my squat and point at a picture on the flap
and then point at myself. The small man laughs.

The small man — he could be you, I decide. I tilt my head up to
him but he doesn't speak so I can understand. Didn't I leave you
years before? A smiling man appears beside him. Him, I know. Son!
Son! His face stricken, he moves away.

We three stand in a room that must be a kitchen, it is so warm. There is something wrong. I have this book — the library gave it to me — and my son is trapped inside, the way I was. The man beside me cups his hand around his ear. What am I saying? I pull the book apart. It does not take long.

BIRD BOY

He —
I am the one to notice — squats behind the can
      riotous with trash, and sings without abash-
ment, as if his
             wants were laid upon the lid, a barmecide
to passersby, imaginary feast, and we appreciate it. We — the
      sidewalk-blind — progress as fantoccini,
         our strings flying, our legs of
wood clattering, *hup to*, his
begging discomfiting, until we — myself, at least – rush out of range.

SYLPH

The creation myth
thinned
to matted hair
and a running stream.

Point of fact:
slime is what makes
the psyllium coat, okra-
green caught / carried off,

and sunlessness so interior
sound goes lipless. *Sylph,* she says,
rises, green clinging, all god,
no -dess for once.

The glade-light practices,
a Klieg advancing
sylvan, a deer forelegged
in adoration,

not the opposite of animal,
the terror of prairie,
what you came from,
mind made.

THE TERRACES AGAINST THE HILLSIDE
SAY IMMORTAL, THE TREES —

The terraces say whatever they say, decay really,
less Man was here than the tree, cabled to the hillside,
the blue of eternity laid between each needle. Beyond me

and the little construct of time and space I occupy, eating
eating eating, my infrared heat, my several single-celled selves
exchanging parasites in the ether around skin and cough

and spoor is the trunk, with its deceit of root and branch
belying its age, leaning on the bare cable. Its evergreen bows
never go bare and the wind against them never dies.

The more sophisticated argue that the cable's current is
equally tree, and so is the smoke at night that makes me weep,
the shed needles in their beds, and the intricate sea.

CRASH-AND-A-HALF

Mourn the poem or porn locked inside or fried,
the white scrambled pre-word,
impulses so electric they're post-, just the paths.

The embarrassment of backup's been forgotten,
Alzheimer put on like a coat you paid a lot for,
months owed to a machine. Here —

take this, my life in numbered bundles.
Don't forget. Such blackness arrives always
sudden and sad but peaceful, not even an accident

this time. And you, half-brained, *mea culpa* the air
where the data hadn't risen to cloud height,
so suitable for burial, disremembered, dismembered.

DEVOURING THE GREEN

Get lyric because the machine will.
Two bits, giga-giggle: the sound-scope Mahler, the picture —

      the big picture. Stand on the ape. Stand up.

The green in the mouth,
          tasted.
     Look down the throat of it.

              Maybe witness, maybe
a bug
that overwinters that winter. Slang spit green
       corrupts, a tongue that just
                    fits that just —
          drive over it.

FLAVOR

should unroll in ten columns of like symbols —
orange orange orange orange orange orange orange orange pink orange

a pixel at a time before mango, then mango picture, no salivating,
mango picture of the past, mango picture of nonexistent fruit,

alleged flavor, which chemical matches mango-like paper,
a mango-like symbol for mango-like paper, paperless mango, not even

the flavor of paper, instead the quiver of, the hint of the synapse orange
orange orange, a burst of electricity said to be by those lightning-hit

bitter, the leap of nanos, orange orange leap orange simile,
simulacra, deep in the cave of, symbol mango symbol.

About the Author

Terese Svoboda is the author of *All Aberration, Laughing Africa, Treason, Mere Mortals,* and *Weapons Grade,* and the chapbook, *Dogs Are Not Cats.*

A recent Guggenheim recipient, she has won the Iowa Prize in Poetry, the Cecil Hemley Award and the Emily Dickinson Prize from the Poetry Society of America, and a New York Foundation for the Arts grant. A fellow at Bellagio, Bogliasco, Yaddo, the James Merrill House, MacDowell, and the NEH, she also received a PEN/Columbia fellowship to translate Nuer song. She has taught at Williams, Columbia's School of the Arts, Southampton/ Stony Brook, the New School, San Francisco State, William and Mary, Fairleigh Dickinson, Sarah Lawrence, Bennington, Atlantic Center for the Arts, and the Universities of Tampa, Miami, and Hawaii, Fordham, and Wichita State, in St. Petersburg and Kenya for the Summer Literary Program, and held the McGee Professor at Davidson College. Also the author of six books of fiction, a memoir, and a book of translation from the Nuer, she will publish a biography of the radical poet Lola Ridge in 2016.